FOUL DEEDS & SUSPICIOUS DEATHS AROUND HULL

FOUL DEEDS AND SUSPICIOUS DEATHS Series

Foul Deeds and Suspicious Deaths series explores in detail crimes of passion, brutal murders, grisly deeds and foul misdemeanours. From Victorian street crime, to more modern murder where passion, jealousy, or social depravation brought unexpected violence to those involved. From mysterious death to murder and manslaughter, the books are a fascinating insight into not only those whose lives are forever captured by the suffering they endured, but also into the society that moulded and shaped their lives. Each book takes you on a journey into the darker and unknown side of the area.

Other titles in the series

Foul Deeds and Suspicious Deaths in Blackburn & Hyndburn,
Steve Greenhalgh.
ISBN: 1-903425-18-2 £9.99

Foul Deeds and Suspicious Deaths in and around Chesterfield, Geoffrey Sadler.
ISBN: 1-903425-30-1 £9.99

Foul Deeds and Suspicious Deaths in & around Durham, Maureen Anderson
ISBN: 1-903425-46-8 £9.99

Foul Deeds and Suspicious Deaths in and around Halifax, Stephen Wade
ISBN: 1-903425-45-X £9.99

Foul Deeds and Suspicious Deaths in Leeds, David Goodman
ISBN: 1-903425-08-5 £9.99

Foul Deeds and Suspicious Deaths in Nottingham, Kevin Turton
ISBN: 1-903425-35-2 £9.99

Foul Deeds and Suspicious Deaths in and around Rotherham, Kevin Turton
ISBN: 1-903425-27-1 £9.99

Foul Deeds and Suspicious Deaths Around the Tees, Maureen Anderson
ISBN: 1-903425-26-3 £9.99

More Foul Deeds and Suspicious Deaths in Wakefield, Kate Taylor
ISBN: 1-903425-48-4 £9.99

Foul Deeds and Suspicious Deaths in York, Keith Henson
ISBN: 1-903425-33-6 £9.99

Foul Deeds and Suspicious Deaths on the Yorkshire Coast, Alan Whitworth
ISBN: 1-903425-01-8 £9.99

Foul Deeds and Suspicious Deaths in Coventry, David McGrory
ISBN: 1-903425-57-3 £9.99

Foul Deeds and Suspicious Deaths in Manchester, Martin Baggoley
ISBN: 1-903425-65-4 £9.99

Foul Deeds and Suspicious Deaths in and Around Newcastle,
Maureen Anderson
ISBN: 1-903425-34-4 £9.99

Foul Deeds and Suspicious Deaths Around Oxfordshire, Carl Boardman
ISBN: 1-903425-56-5 £9.99

Foul Deeds and Suspicious Deaths Around Pontefract and Castleford,
Keith Henson
ISBN: 1-903425-54-9 £9.99

Foul Deeds & Suspicious Deaths Around

HULL

DAVID GOODMAN

Series Editor
Brian Elliott

Wharncliffe Books

First published in Great Britain in 2005
and reprinted in 2015 by
WHARNCLIFFE BOOKS
An imprint of
Pen & Sword Books Ltd
47 Church Street
Barnsley, South Yorkshire
S70 2AS

ISBN 978 1 90342 543 5

A CIP catalogue record for this book is
available from the British Library

Typeset in 11/13pt by
Andy Hemingway, Barnsley, South Yorkshire

Printed and bound in England
By CPI Group (UK) Ltd, Croydon, CR0 4YY

Pen & Sword Books Ltd incorporates the Imprints of Aviation, Atlas,
Family History, Fiction, Maritime, Military, Discovery, Politics, History,
Archaeology, Select, Wharncliffe Local History, Wharncliffe True Crime,
Military Classics, Wharncliffe Transport, Leo Cooper, The Praetorian Press,
Remember When, Seaforth Publishing and Frontline Publishing.

For a complete list of Pen & Sword titles please contact
PEN & SWORD BOOKS LIMITED
47 Church Street, Barnsley, South Yorkshire, S70 2AS, England
E-mail: enquiries@pen-and-sword.co.uk
Website: www.pen-and-sword.co.uk

Contents

Introduction

Researching among the local papers of the day for Hull *Foul Deeds and Suspicious Deaths*, it struck me quite what a violent place Hull appeared to be in Victorian times! For a time, especially towards the end of Victoria's reign, there appeared to be a murder almost every other week in the city, whilst other assaults, suicides and other acts of violence were almost too numerous to mention.

Perhaps it was not such a surprise as Hull, during the late nineteenth and early twentieth century, established itself as one of the world's leading ports, an integral part of the Industrial Revolution. However, this success came at a cost.

The public health of the city suffered due to the population expanding at an alarming rate. In Hull the population rose from 22,000 in 1801 to 239,000 in 1901. The problems of poverty and overcrowding were not helped by the large numbers of people coming into the city from surrounding areas looking for work. Houses were built quickly, close together, and disease was rife.

Therefore, crime was a big problem in Hull, possibly more so than cities of a similar size and some of the most noteworthy are recorded in this book with Hull's status as a leading port making an interesting backdrop.

The first chapter, the death of William Pepper, a young fisherboy, occurred on a Hull fishing smack out in the North Sea, whilst in most of the other chapters, the victim, killer or both are likely to be in jobs on or related to the docks.

In addition, several unsolved murders are featured and, though nobody has ever been charged, in more than once case, the body was found on a site near to the docks and prime suspects included people who had made a fleeting visit to Hull on board a ship. This, once again, highlights the difficulties that the police in Hull may have had compared to other forces with many more temporary visitors in Hull than elsewhere.

Hull's unique character at this time made this book fascinating to research and I hope that each chapter gives a little flavour of the period in which the crime occurred. I hope also that each case is of interest. Aside from William Pepper, I have researched the case of William George Smith; most interesting because of the impact it had on the city for a time. I have also devoted a chapter to Frederick Bailey Deeming, not a Hull man, nor were any of his victims from the city, but he does have a strong Hull connection which makes him eligible for selection.

In addition, there are other intriguing cases including a man murdering his daughter and attempting to kill another whilst there is the tragic story of a mother beheading her baby daughter. I found all the cases interesting to research and I hope and believe they are worthy of re-telling.

There are many people I have to thank for their assistance in the research of his book. Firstly, David Smith and the rest of the staff at the Local Studies Library at Hull Central Library. David could not have been more helpful and was very enthusiastic about the project. I spent several days in the library and all of them were usefully spent.

I would also like to thank Chris Ketchell at the Hull College Local History Unit for the photographs that he gave me permission to use. I was especially grateful as Chris is such an authority on local history in Hull and is always a pleasure to deal with.

Brian Elliott and all at Wharncliffe Books also warrant my thanks for always being on call to answer my queries and not putting too much pressure on me to finish the book on time!

Finally, I would like to thank my dad for his own interest in postcards. He has quite a collection, including many superb ones from Hull, and I am grateful for his permission to publish some of them in this book.

In conclusion, I have thoroughly enjoyed writing this book. I was perhaps helped by the fact that I have a great affinity and love for the city of Hull. Though the subject matter is necessarily rather gruesome, I found it fascinating to read about the conditions in which people lived in the back streets of Hull at the turn of the last century and how, in some extreme cases, their lives were transformed by evil acts. I hope and believe it to be a worthy addition to the bookshelves.

CHAPTER 1

Murder in the North Sea
1881

Even on Christmas Day, Pepper went without food.

The fisherboys, as they came to be known, were young boys, without homes in many cases, who worked on the many trawlers from Hull and Grimsby which scoured the North Sea for fish to take back to port. It involved arduous work, often including routine beatings and abuse whilst at sea and, once back on dry land, the boys were often left to fend for themselves until it was once again time for their boat to sail out onto the cold waters of the North Sea. Prostitution, hard drinking and violence were common threads running through their young lives and, perhaps unsurprisingly, there were a high number of suicides in their midst.

William Pepper, occasionally known as Papper, was one such fisherboy. He got a job working on the *Rising Sun*, a wooden

Russian fire on the Hull fishing fleet, showing the persistent danger to the trawlers. Author's collection

The Victoria Docks at the end of the nineteenth century. Author's collection

fishing smack, which was regularly used in the fishing trade. The Pepper household lived, as so many involved in the fishing trade did, near to Hessle Road but on Chiltern Street, at the poorer end. William's father used to make a living by 'coaling' the fishing boats and other craft. Having worked in his father's coal business, Pepper, aged fourteen, was a slight boy but was strong for his size and well used to hard, physical work. He was known to many in the community as a cheerful boy and an obedient shipmate.

The skipper and part-owner of the *Rising Sun* was Osmond Otto Brand, a twenty-seven-year-old man from Hull, who lived on Staniforth Place, at the more salubrious end of Hessle Road. It was a respectable neighbourhood and the house was nicely furnished, though Brand was perhaps regretting his decision to invest in the smack as he was in debt throughout most of 1881.

Whilst in Hull between voyages, Pepper used to stay at Brand's house rather than with his parents. He was serving, what was usually regarded as a seven-year apprenticeship with the skipper. As well as being the cook on trips, he was also expected to help in the hauling up of the trawl by hand. As soon as fish were caught and hauled up, they would be packed in ice and stored until the cargo was ready to be returned to port.

The *Rising Sun* sailed out from the Albert Dock in Hull a couple of weeks before Christmas 1881 before dropping anchor at Sunk Island, near Spurn Point. The crew consisted of Brand as skipper, William Dench as second hand, Frederick Ryecroft as third hand, William Blackburn, a spare hand, David

Yates, a deck boy and William Pepper as the ship's cook.

Brand had tolerated Pepper rather than liked him, but there was no hint of the trouble that lay ahead when the *Rising Sun* left Hull. Pepper had been the last on board and on his arrival he was keen to tell Brand that, having spoken to his sister Emma, Pepper found out that she knew Brand.

For some unexplained reason this infuriated Brand who exploded at the remark, saying, 'Now you, I'll pay you for telling lies about me.'

As the smack proceeded towards its first destination, Brand continued to fume at the remark, becoming ever more offensive towards the boy, claiming, falsely, that he had slept with Pepper's sister, and then abusing Pepper physically. The young boy was tied to the side of the boat, whilst Brand threw buckets of cold water over him before punching him to the ground.

The *Rising Sun* reached Sunk Island at about seven o'clock in the evening and cast anchor. The beatings had been continuing intermittently throughout the day and they carried on through the evening. Brand began hitting Pepper with a ratliner, the end of which was weighted with pieces of iron. To justify this, he accused the boy of badly arranging the core nets so making the previous cast a failure. This allegation also turned the rest of the crew against Pepper as a bad cast would affect their earnings.

Half an hour later, Brand told Pepper to get some lacing to tie the main sail. The boy went below deck but the skipper followed him and started shouting and accusing him of spreading lies. Pepper replied; 'I never said so', but Brand persisted, getting a rope out and, holding the boy by the shoulders, thrashed him about the head and face. After about five minutes he was then heard to say to the boy, 'Now, go and get washed.'

Throughout the next few days, Brand continued to assault Pepper including knocking him to the ground before jumping on top of him. He also seized a rope and tied it around the boy's neck until he struggled for breath. He shouted at Pepper, 'Now you, say your prayers, because you won't live another day on board this smack.'

By Friday, 23 December, the boat had sailed about ninety miles off Spurn Point. At about nine o'clock in the morning Dench was on the deck, helping to mend the trawl line whilst Brand and Pepper were also about. Dench witnessed Brand punch Pepper in the face, knocking him down. The net sustained damage in the process and Brand shouted at Pepper, 'You, that is all through you'. He continued to hit Pepper who by now was crying. Then Brand grabbed hold of a bucket, filled it with seawater and threw it over the boy. In total he threw about ten buckets of water over the boy until Dench intervened, restraining Brand who was threatening to kill Pepper and tear his liver out.

As well as physical beatings, Pepper was also being starved. He was only given water and broken biscuits during his time on the boat and even this was scarce. The rest of the crew ate well but the boy was even reduced to eating raw skate from part of the catch on one occasion.

Even on Christmas Day, Pepper went without food. He remained on deck whilst the rest of the crew tucked into duck, beef, potatoes and plum pudding. For a moment Brand seemed to take pity on the boy and put some of his pudding on a fork, holding it out for Pepper to take. Yet, as the boy reached out to take the food, Brand rapped him across the knuckles with a stick and fed him a single currant. The duck bones were given to the ship's dog rather than Pepper, who was hungry enough to gnaw at them when the dog had finished.

Artist's impression of Brand attacking Pepper. Hull News

At half past seven on the morning of 29 December, the crew hauled their trawl in and saw there was a hole in the net. Brand told Pepper, who by now was in a very weakened state to, 'Be sharp and fill some needles and you shall have some dinner.' Pepper did as he was told, filling in all the holes before being given a single dumpling which he ate quickly.

However, there was to be no softening of Brand's attitude to his young charge and, having ordered Pepper back on deck, he began to throw more buckets of water over him. After completely drenching the boy with about a dozen buckets of water, he ordered the young boy to get to his feet. Pepper replied, 'Don't throw any more and I'll get up, Brand said, 'Get up then.' Pepper did so, but with difficulty and he began to have trouble breathing.

Later that same day, 29 December, Brand took a handspike from a small boat that was on deck and went up to Pepper, handing the handspike to him, at the same time putting the big end on the rail. He then forced Pepper to sing out at the top of his voice, 'If I had not been a bad lad I should not have had to do this, cuckoo.' Brand also gave Pepper some new clothes to wear as he was soaking wet. He was given a fresh pair of stockings and a new shirt to wear, but he could not get the stockings on as he was so cold and wet, though he managed to get his shirt on. Brand barked at him to get the stockings on but Pepper was unable to.

In anger Brand got a piece of rattling line out of the wing, about half an inch thick and told him that if he didn't get his stockings on he would receive a good thrashing. Pepper did not reply and Brand started beating him on the back with the piece of line. By this time Pepper's eyes were blackened, his lips swollen and the rest of his body was covered in bruises. Brand handed Dench a rope down into the hole and told him to tie it round Pepper and then haul him up. Once this was done Pepper was slung onto the deck where Ryecroft threw a bucket of water over him. When Blackburn brought another bucket of water onto deck, Ryecroft took out some excrement and smeared it over Pepper's face and mouth.

After about twenty minutes, Brand ordered Dench and Blackburn to throw yet more water over the helpless boy while he was lashed to the rail. Ryecroft then put a line around Pepper's waist before shoving him into the dill. Pepper said 'God help me' and started crying. Brand then jumped down below and stood on Pepper's shoulders while the boy was in a kneeling position. The fog bell was hanging in the rigging and just then it rang out, Brand said to Pepper 'There you, there's the bell tolling for your death.'

Leaving Pepper lying on deck, Brand went to have some dinner with the rest of the crew, but half an hour later, Dench came back onto deck and saw Pepper lying there on his back, his eyes and face black. Dench thought he may have fainted and put a little water on his face to try and revive him but there was no response. He rushed down to the cabin and told Brand that he thought Pepper was dying. However, Brand appeared not to care, replying, 'And a good thing too. We can't take him back to Hull because his face is disfigured.' Ryecroft and Blackburn came onto deck and carried Pepper below.

By now the boy was unconscious and Brand, belatedly, began to realise the gravity of the situation. He told his men to go and get some old canvas to put on the warp, adding 'we will sew him up and throw him overboard, he's only shamming.' They got the canvas, spread it out and laid Pepper in it on the state room floor. They then dangled him overboard whilst he was wrapped in the canvas but it had no effect. Back on deck they also shoved tobacco and tea down his throat, but it was all to no avail and they doubled the canvas over, leaving the boy there overnight, perhaps hoping that when they awoke, Pepper would somehow have been revived.

William Pepper. Hull College Local Studies Unit

Brand woke up first the next morning and saw that Pepper was dead. He took the body out of the state room and laid it in a cabin. Dench woke up at about six to see Brand standing over him, informing him that Pepper had died in the night. Brand said to Dench 'Well, what are we to do now'? Dench replied 'I don't know, he's our apprentice.'

Brand immediately went on the defensive claiming that the whole crew were as guilty as he was. All of them then hatched a plot to make it look as though the boy had accidentally been knocked overboard during the night by one of the sails caught in the wind. So Brand and the rest of the crew covered the body in the canvas before throwing it into the sea.

David Yates, the deckhand, was the only one of the crew who was unaware of the events and was told by Brand that a tragedy had occurred and that Pepper had accidentally fallen into the sea and drowned.

The *Rising Sun* arrived back in Hull on 5 January and William Pepper's father was at the dockside ready to welcome his son back onto dry land. Brand broke the news to him that his son was dead, making a passable impression of a distressed and sympathetic man, before going on to the police station in Parliament Street to make a statement. It read:

The old police station in Parliament Street. The author

> *I report that at about 5.30 am on January 1 1882 we were trawling on the fishing ground around 120 miles from Spurn when the cook William Pepper 14 years of age and a native of Hull, was knocked overboard (and drowned) by the big foresail ship. The smack was put about and every effort was made to save him but without avail.*

It appeared to be a tragic accident and nothing more was publicly heard of the case for some time and Brand and the rest of the crew got on with their lives. However, the skipper knew that there were constant whispers from people in Hull that the death was no accident. The Pepper family in particular appeared to be unhappy with Brand's version of events and were beginning to feel that he had more of an involvement in the death than was first thought. In particular they had heard claims that Brand had mistreated their son whilst on board the vessel and put two and two together.

The crew were also hearing the rumours and were reaching the point where, either through guilt or in an attempt to save themselves, they felt a duty to report what went on whilst the *Rising Sun* was out at sea. Eventually, Blackburn and Yates visited the home of James Campbell, Hull's Chief Constable and made a statement regarding what happened to William Pepper with Dench coming along later to also give a statement.

Armed with this information the police arrested Brand and took him back to the police station in Parliament Street where he was formally charged with the wilful murder of William Pepper. On being charged, Brand replied to the police officer, 'There were three of us in it.'

Copy of return of Fisherboys who died at sea between January 1878 and September 1882. Hull College

,,	17	William Knapman	20	John Brown	,,	,, ,,
November	27	George Houghton	18	Bessie Lewis	,,	Taking in the jib and washed overboard by heavy sea.
,,	30	Thomas Chapman	16	Alethia	,,	Reefing the topsail and fell overboard.
December	19	Henry Silby	18	Magic	,,	Washed overboard by heavy sea.
,,	,,	Alfred Foster	14	Speedwell	,,	,, ,,
,,	,,	George Holmes	16	Sir Joseph	,,	,, ,,
1882.						
✱ January	1	William Papper	14	Rising Sun	,,	Knocked overboard by the sail.
,,	6	Joseph Clinton	20	William	,,	Washed overboard by heavy sea.
,,	7	August Fallengberg	19	Olive-branch	,,	Putting the top lift right and fell overboard.
,,	10	John W. Foster	18	Albert	,,	Washed overboard by heavy sea.
,,	,,	George Cooper	17	Winter	,,	,, ,,
,,	19	George Camby	17	Hope	,,	Drawing a bucket of water and fell overboard.
February	13	John Ridley	20	Regulea	Killed	Struck by handle of winch, when heaving the gear, and killed.
,,	18	Richard Gorbeckett	18	Loch Long	Drowned	Reefing the sail and blown overboard.
,,	24	Peter Hoye	16	Gleaner	,,	Drawing a bucket of water and fell overboard.

Brand was initially remanded for eight days and the following day, he was up before the police court to frenzied media interest. The case generally aroused great interest in Hull and also Grimsby, which had its own community of fisher boys. There was such curiosity that, in anticipation, the Chief Constable had to employ extra police in the vicinity of the Town Hall to try and maintain order. He also ensured that the witnesses were lodged at the central police station for the duration of the trial.

For the hearing, Brand was taken from jail to the Town Hall in a taxi and a huge crowd started shouting and gesturing as soon as the vehicle entered Lowgate. He was rushed into the building and down into the cells.

A reporter from the *Hull Daily Mail* noted:

> *Brand was brought in by Detective Superintendent Trafford. He was a smart little fellow and was well liked by the whole fishing community. If he's been guilty of half the acts which were alleged against him he was one of the most heartless of men but certainly his manner did not convey that impression.*

The Town Hall (now the Guildhall) on Lowgate. The author

Brand was committed for trial at the next York Assizes but spent time on remand at the Hedon Road Gaol in Hull from where he made a daring bid to escape just days before the trial was due to start. He succeeded in making a hole in the wall which looked onto the adjacent cemetery and had the hole not been discovered in time, he would almost certainly have been able to escape and cause great embarrassment to the prison authorities in the process.

Brand pleaded not guilty to murder at his trial but with Dench, and the rest of the crew testifying against him, the jury took just seven minutes to find him guilty of murder. He was sentenced to death by Mr Justice Williams, who told him:

> *In all my personal experience and from all my reading of the state of crime in this country, I have never read a crime of greater atrocity than that of which the jury have convicted you.*

Having been found guilty of the crime, Brand had become one of the country's most notorious murderers with the *Hull Times* describing his crime as a murder 'almost without parallel in the annals of English crime.'

The revulsion felt by the community at large did not limit itself solely to Brand. The other crew members were deemed guilty by association and had a difficult time back in their home city. William Dench, who had given key evidence against Brand at his trial netherthess faced a demonstration when he returned to his home in Staniforth Place, Hessle Road, just a few doors away from Brand's home. A large crowd of fishermen who were angry at his part in the death of Pepper gathered and threatened him with violence. Though the atmosphere was ugly for a time, police were eventually called to restore order.

Amongst the tight-knit fishing community of Hull there was shock and anger at the news of the murder and Brand's subsequent conviction. There was revulsion at such crime going on aboard a working vessel. One said:

> *His conduct was a disgrace to all sailors; but he's to be punished, and that is all we care about. We only want to forget all about it and not to remember that Brand was ever one of us.*

Armley Gaol in its early days. West Yorkshire Archive Service

Such was the widespread feeling over the crime that with the death sentence having been passed on Brand, there were, unusually, no petitions or calls for a reprieve. After being sentenced to death, Brand spent the rest of his days in the condemned cell at Armley Gaol in Leeds where he was due to be executed.

In his last few days, incarcerated in the condemned cell, Brand had apparently lost his fear of death and seemed to almost look forward to the end. He was remarkably cool but the same could not be said of his wife who protested his innocence to the end and visited him regularly in Armley. She fainted at their last meeting, devastated at the thought that it would be the last time she saw him alive.

Brand's last evening in prison was spent writing a final letter to his wife. He also wrote a long statement on the crime and the circumstances around it. He handed this to the prison governor on the understanding that it would eventually be sent to the Home Secretary. In the statement he tried to lay the blame for the death elsewhere and said that his conduct towards the boy was acceptable, stressing that Pepper was never deprived of food the whole time he was on the ship.

He said that he had thrashed Pepper with the lacing he had

been sent for, but that subsequently the boy had been beaten by Dench and William Blackburn. He then alleged that Pepper had not obeyed him in carrying out some tasks and that was the reason he was being punished. On Boxing Day he saw Dench, Blackburn and Ryecroft throwing water over the young man and later witnessed Blackburn putting some dirt into Pepper's mouth. He said that Pepper went to him for protection and he stopped the others ill-treating the boy.

He said that on another occasion, when he saw Blackburn hitting the boy and throwing water over him, he intervened, claiming that Ryecroft had told him that Dench and Blackburn would kill the boy if they persisted in abusing him. They reportedly replied, 'Bloody good job; he wanted killing out of the road.'

He then claimed that Dench and Blackburn ignored the warning and continued to ill-treat Pepper, throwing water over him and causing him to have several cuts to his face. They caused such injuries that Pepper was left lying on the deck of the *Rising Sun*, apparently unconscious.

On the night of Pepper's death, Brand said that he, along with Ryecroft and Dench went down to dinner whilst Blackburn stayed on deck. Ryecroft later went on deck and said that the boy was dead but Brand claimed that they thought they saw signs of life and tried to revive him by undressing him and putting him in front of the fire. However, they eventually realised that there was nothing they could do for Pepper and thoughts turned to disposing of the body.

Brand went on:

> *We then agreed to bury the boy at sea, which we did and it was sanctioned that I should make the report at the police station, as stated at the trial, which I did, to save them from getting into trouble, but to my sorrow, as it has turned out, and I can assure you that Dench and Blackburn is the boy's murderers, and not me, neither Ryecroft.*
>
> *I have had nine boys and not one of them can say that I have ill-used them, neither have I ever had a flaw against my character for the seven years I have been in command, neither before, and I trust that the public feeling will have a great change towards my poor wife, and thank God I shall leave*

> *this world with a clear conscience of this foul deed which I am about to suffer for, as the country has doomed me to go through.*

Brand alleged that Dench did not want to return home after assisting in throwing the body into the water as it would lead to all of them getting into trouble. He added, 'We have all put nails in his coffin'. Blackburn also wanted to stay out at sea, but Brand and Ryecroft were prepared to go home to face the music and the skipper decided that was what they must do.

It was a lengthy statement from Brand, but his comments cut little ice and he remained on death row. Whilst in Armley Gaol, however, he did manage to create a favourable impression amongst the prison staff.

The *Hull & Lincolnshire Times* reported:

> *The prisoner has left behind him at Armley the reputation of being a man of amiable disposition and utterly unlike the hard-hearted, callous individual who would be likely to be guilty of such an appalling crime.*

The scaffold at Armley had been erected in its usual place, on the south side of the prison, adjoining the B wing exercising ground where Brand's grave had already been dug and shortly before eight o'clock on the Tuesday morning, 23 May 1882, the procession began from inside Armley Gaol. There was a general murmur amongst the spectators as a bald-headed and pinioned Brand first came into public view.

When Brand reached the scaffold he turned to where Mr Keene, the prison governor, was standing. He whispered his thanks for the kindness he had received in the prison during his last few days of life, before climbing the steps and placing

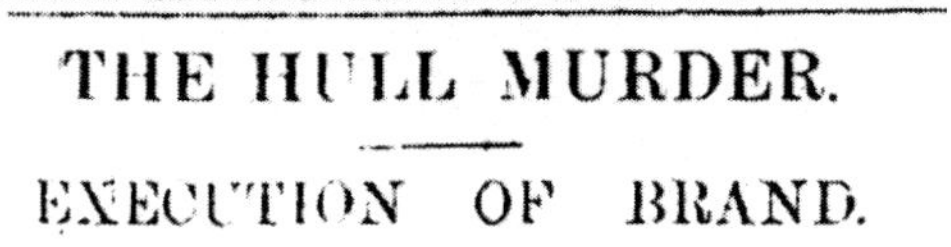
MAY 27, 1882

THE HULL MURDER.

EXECUTION OF BRAND.

Newspaper headline featuring the execution of Otto Brand. Hull Times himself in position upon the drop. Once the drop was released, death was instantaneous and a black flag was raised to give a signal to the outside world that Brand had died.

The body was allowed to hang for an hour until it was moved to one of the cells for the inquest to be held and it was eventually buried within the precincts of the prison.

His death signalled the end of an inglorious chapter in Hull's history. Of the many murders in the city during Victorian times, the killing of William Pepper ranks as perhaps the most infamous. Brand's death did not, of course, mark an end to the suffering of the Pepper family and Pepper's father, in particular, was badly affected by his son's death, sadly entering into conversation about it for long periods, sometimes with total strangers.

Brand's wife, who remained in Hull after his execution was also grieving and even after his death, spoke up on his behalf. She felt that her late husband was incapable of killing anyone in such a brutal manner and she was afforded some sympathy by the fishing community in Hull which felt that in a way she had also been a victim of the crime. To add to her woes, Brand had been heavily in debt at the time of his arrest and whilst he was in prison his house was sold in order to settle some of these arrears.

There was also great hostility to the other members of the crew on board the *Rising Sun*. The *Hull and Lincolnshire Times* reported:

> *I should not like to repeat the expressions applied to those mariners when their names were mentioned, and should any of them appear in the Hull Billinsgate at an early period a mauvais quart d'heure indeed would be the result.*

Sensing the mood, the remaining crew were not to stay in Hull much longer. All of them soon left the city, unable to face the hostility they received from the fishing people as well as the wider community. Dench fled to London at the conclusion of the trial, Ryecroft was soon spending time at his majesties pleasure in Wakefield for other offences whilst Blackburn and Yates, returned to their original homes in the thriving colliery district of Bolton in Lancashire.

The murder of Pepper reached the national headlines as well as dominating the local ones and led to a far-reaching investigation into the fishing industry's apprentice system. The fisherboys became the subject of new legislation but the growth of larger fishing firms towards the end of the nineteenth century eventually signalled the demise of the apprentice system anyway.

A pub in North Hull ensures that the name of The Rising Sun *lives on in the city.* The author

CHAPTER 2

A City Protests
1924

She fell over the doorstop,
the front of her clothing covered in blood...

Elizabeth Bousefield was a twenty-eight-year-old married woman with three children. She married her husband in wartime, but almost immediately he went off to serve in a regiment abroad and due to the fact that they spent so little time together, the couple separated; though they remained friends and were in regular contact, mainly for the sake of the children.

Since the separation, Bousefield and the children had lived with eighty-year-old Thomas Senior, a coal trimmer, and his nephew, George Barber, in Arundel Street off Holderness Road. Bousefield was working as Senior's live-in housekeeper.

She had recently begun a friendship with William George

The East Hull area where Arundel Street was situated. The turning on the right indicates where it was until recent demolition.
The author

Smith, a young ship's painter and chipper. Aged twenty-six, Smith had served in the Great War between 1916 and 1919 and first met Bousefield in the autumn of 1922 when they were at a football match. He was living at home with his mother at the time and during Christmas 1922 he and his mother were invited to Senior's house and all four of them became friends. From then on Smith visited Senior's house almost every day.

He spent more and more time there, often playing cards and spending hours chatting to Senior and Bousefield before going back home to sleep. Annie Tallon, Smith's mother, began to suspect that the attractive Bousefield was more of a lure to her son than Senior and she told Smith that the time had come when he must choose between the woman and his home.

After a lengthy argument with his mother, Smith decided to pack his bags and he went to stay at the nearby Victoria Mansions. This arrangement saw him go to Arundel Street for his breakfast and other meals where Bousefield would also pack him a meal for the following lunchtime before he headed off back to Victoria Mansions to sleep.

Bousefield had confided in Smith, telling him how unhappy her married life had been and that she had left her husband in order to come to Hull. She told him that if only she could get someone to look after her, she would be all right. Smith was looking for such an invitation and readily agreed to this. They made plans and appeared on the verge of moving in together and getting engaged once Bousefield's divorce could be finalised. They both approached Senior, telling him of their plans. He replied, 'Well Bill, you are taking a big thing on with three children to look after.'

On 13 August 1924, Smith spent the Wednesday evening with both Bousefield and Senior, the three of them going to the cinema together. Smith had never stayed at the house before but when they returned to Arundel Street after seeing the film, he said to Senior, 'I should like to stop here for the night, I don't feel like going. Can I have a shake-down'? Senior agreed and Smith settled down for the night on the couch in the kitchen.

When Smith retired to bed, Bousefield went upstairs with Senior following her. Senior said, 'Come on Liz my old love' and then, according to Smith, made an obscene remark before following her upstairs. They all went their separate ways to bed and later, Senior's nephew came back and went to bed in the same room as Senior. The following morning he went to work, leaving Bousefield and Smith in the kitchen, apparently on good terms together and Senior still in bed.

Bousefield, who shared her bedroom with all three of her children, had got up early to go into the kitchen to make some lunch for Smith to take to work as usual. Smith woke up on hearing her and asked her about the remarks Senior had made the night before. She admitted that Senior had made them and got quite upset, beginning to cry.

Smith continued pressing her about her relationship with Senior, but she was still upset and Smith was left confused as to whether there was any sort of relationship, despite it appearing unlikely, between Bousefield and Senior. He went into the yard before going to work and when he returned inside she was still crying. He asked her what was wrong and she replied that she could not help what had happened between her and 'the old man' as she referred to him.

Smith tried to placate her, suggesting that the only way they could progress as a couple was to get a place together, away from Senior. This seemed to settle Bousefield and a little later she was seen by neighbours appearing quite happy, singing and joking with those around her.

However, that was the last time she was seen alive as just a few minutes later, at about quarter to eight on the Thursday morning, Bousefield was found with her throat cut and a bloodstained razor lying nearby, indicating the weapon which had been used.

Other neighbours came out on hearing the commotion and saw Bousefield staggering at the doorway before collapsing. She fell over the doorstep, the front of her clothing covered in blood, her head and body on the pavement and her legs inside the house. The neighbours quickly reached her but she was already beyond help.

Mary Crowther, who lived nearby, on looking out of her window, saw Bousefield leaning against the door of her house before sinking to the ground. She saw that blood was running from her throat which appeared to have been cut.

Mrs Garrad, who was walking down Arundel Street at the time the incident occurred, saw three children crying outside number 86 and a minute or two later noticed that a man rushed out of the house in his shirtsleeves and disappeared down the street.

The neighbours called for an ambulance but Elizabeth Bousefield was already dead by the time doctors rushed to the scene. She had a large wound in her neck across her throat, five inches in length and extending to a depth of two inches. It had come through several muscles and had severed an artery and the jugular vein.

After the attack, Smith darted out the house and ran down Arundel Street in the direction of Craven Street Bridge. A man called Moore was seated near the boards at the corner of Arundel Street eating his breakfast on that Thursday morning. He heard a disturbance further up the street and saw a man running down the street with his coat off and without his collar and hat. Smith shouted to Moore, 'Have you seen a policeman?' Moore replied, 'No, I haven't' and Smith continued running, turning the corner and going out of sight.

He ran all the way to the Crowle Street police station where he told officers, 'I have cut a woman's throat, will you arrest

Craven Street today. The author

me?' He told the officers questioning him that Bousefield was still in the house as far as he was aware.

Superintendent Cocksworth sent PC Askern along with an ambulance to the house in Arundel Street along with Inspector Foster. Dr Walker was already there when the police arrived and was able to confirm to them that the woman was dead. Her body was removed to the mortuary and the three children were temporarily placed into the care of Annie Tallon, a strange decision considering that her son was the prime suspect, indeed the only suspect for the murder.

The noise and general commotion failed to rouse Thomas Senior who was very deaf and heard no scream or any other noise to indicate that a struggle had taken place. Indeed, he was still in bed when police came to the house, and they had to break the news to him that his housekeeper had been murdered whilst he slept.

After Smith had handed himself over to the police, he gave a statement in which he wrongly claimed that he had been living at the house with Bousefield and her uncle for about two years. The officers soon charged him with the wilful murder of Elizabeth Bousefield.

He was remanded in custody and came up before Hull police court on the Friday morning. He was also present for the inquest into the death of Elizabeth Bousefield which was opened by the city coroner Colonel Thorney before a jury at the mortuary on the Friday afternoon.

Thomas Senior told the inquest that Bousefield's husband was away on duty with his regiment and was believed to be in the Channel Islands. When asked if he cohabited with the dead woman, he replied, 'Never, at any time, no. The woman was my daughter.' He said that the suggestion was the most abominable lie that was ever uttered.

Smith was committed for trial on a coroner's warrant to York Assizes and before being taken down to the cells, gave a glance at his mother, sitting behind him in court who cried, 'God help you my son.'

The attack fascinated those in the neighbourhood of Arundel Street, who were never afraid to give their opinions to the reporters who flocked into the area for a few days afterwards.

Most believed the murder to be the result of an illicit friendship and had heard the news that Smith's mother had apparently given her son an ultimatum of either giving up the woman or leaving home.

Annie Tallon added to the intrigue in the case by talking to the local papers, confirming that Smith was a friend of the dead woman and used to call to see her. She said that he had left home three weeks ago and she had not spoken to him since. She said:

> *I am absolutely astounded but I am not going to let it get the better of me. I am going to face it. I suppose if my son has done it he will have to suffer the penalty.*

Whilst in prison, awaiting trial, Smith gave his side of the story, admitting killing Bousefield, but denying that it was a premeditated murder, saying it was self-defence. He said that on the morning of the attack, he had asked Bousefield whether she considered that he needed a shave. She said he did and he took a razor and put it beside her as she was sitting near a looking glass. He got some hot water and said to her, 'I wonder how it is that women cannot keep straight.' He then alleged that Bousefield:

> *Took up the razor and rushed at me saying 'I will cut your throat'. I seized her by getting one arm around her waist and twisting her wrist to make her drop the razor. When I got the razor she was slipping to the floor. I had a blood-stained razor in my hand and I then noticed there was blood on her throat. I put down the razor and went straight to the police.*
>
> *Before I knew what I was doing I saw red on her throat. The razor seemed to come into my hand and it was done before I knew what I was doing. I never intended to hurt her for I worshipped the ground she walks on. If it had been a young man I would have given way for him. I must have slashed at her boots as the razor was gabbed, if not I would have done myself in. I'm sorry it has happened but I suppose it must be God's work.*

Mr Burnand, defending Smith in his subsequent trial at York Assizes, said he was sure the jury would agree that this was one of the saddest cases they had ever heard. It was a tragic end to what was for some months a period of love between the two people who planned to be living together and was ended by this tragedy.

He said he was sure that the jury would not be influenced by the fact that Smith had not released the whole of the incident to the officer at the station upon his arrest as the state of his mind at the time must have been terrible.

The jury retired at a quarter to two in the afternoon and returned after half an hour's absence, announcing a verdict of guilty. The judge donned the black cap and, addressing Smith, said that the jury had found him guilty on evidence that had left them with no alternative.

'For the crime of murder the law of England appointed one punishment and one only, namely death. You must therefore die'. The palpable sense of shock around the courtroom was punctuated by the sound of Smith's mother weeping uncontrollably. She shouted at the judge and Smith protested that he had killed the woman he loved because she had been unfaithful to the bond between them.

Outside in the courtyard, a group of people soon congregated in the hope of catching a last glimpse of the prisoner as he was taken from court to the condemned cell at Hull Prison. They were soon rewarded as Smith shortly left the court building in the presence of wardens before being driven in a cab from York Castle back to Hull.

York Castle Debtors' prison. York Castle Museum

The death sentence caused outrage in the city of Hull with few expecting the judge to fix the most severe penalty. A mood of anger quickly swept Hull, fuelled by editorials in the *Hull Daily Mail* and other newspapers condemning the judge's ruling.

The public were confused because another man was tried at York Assizes a day later, in the same court before the same judge. Cornelius Hines had killed his wife, Lilian, in the small house they shared off Tomlinson Street. On the face of it the two cases had incredible coincidences; a married woman with her throat cut by a razor, the accused giving himself up to police and allegations of impropriety between the woman and another man living in the same house.

However, Justice Talbot, twenty-four hours after condemning Smith to death by hanging, sentenced Hines to ten years in jail and said:

> *I am conscious of the grief and pain you must have suffered. I believe you would give everything you possess to undo what you have done.*

The difference in the ruling was put down to the fact that Hines was a happily married man, whilst Smith had killed a woman who was still married to someone else. Smith's attack was put down to unfounded jealousy whilst Hines actions were given some form of justification by his wife's admission of an affair.

However, this did not satisfy the many who wanted the Home Secretary to overturn the conviction. An incredible 86,000 people, almost ninety per cent of the adult population of Hull, signed a petition which was sent to the Home Secretary calling for the reprieve of Smith. The grounds for the petition were Smith's youth, the absence of premeditation and his previous good character. The petition also stated that the crime was committed solely on the grounds of provocation caused by Bousefield's admission leading him to lose all self-control.

However, the Home Secretary decided that there were insufficient grounds to reconsider the verdict and so the death

Hull Gaol soon after it was built in 1870. Hull Local Studies Library

penalty remained. His ruling caused a sensation in the city and a large-scale campaign continued on Smith's behalf. One Sunday afternoon and evening in December a large open-air meeting was held as a protest against the decision and to provide a last-ditch effort to save the life of Smith. Before the meeting a large crowd formed a procession and marched to Hull jail three miles away. Speeches were delivered at the gates of the prison, hymns were sung and the leader of the crowd spoke out, saying they were seeking justice for the condemned man and that if a reprieve was not forthcoming, every working man in the city should down tools and cease work.

However, despite the intensity with which the protests took place, the Home Secretary reiterated his decision that the death sentence stood. It was a crushing blow to many in Hull who felt it was a decision made in London without any local knowledge of the case. Whatever the rights and wrongs, the protestors were forced to conceded that the Home Secretary had delivered his final word and there was little point in continuing with their protests.

Smith's mother, Annie Tallon, felt compelled to respond to the support showed towards her son by many in the city. She said:

My son has been helped by the lowest to the highest people in Hull. His death will not be due to lack of friends and support. They have shown kindness which we can never repay. I know he's grateful for it. The last thing he said to me when I left the prison today was 'do not forget to thank everybody.

Smith was said to have coped with the inevitability of his death quite well, despite having his hopes raised by the protests. He had found consolation in prayer and was said to have found the experience valuable in having brought him nearer to God. He saw his mother in the late afternoon on 8 December, the day before his execution and asked her to thank the public for their support. The emotional visit was brought to an end when his mother said her last words to him, 'Good night laddie, sleep well.'

Smith was executed at Hedon Gaol on 9 December 1924 with Pierrepoint, the executioner, assisted by Baxter. It was carried out at nine o'clock in the morning but due to the controversy, the executioners had arrived at the gaol overnight, under the cover of darkness. In addition, about a hundred policemen were stationed at the gaol during the night in case of further protests and by the early morning a crowd of about 4,000 had gathered, some to continue to protest and others, merely to watch.

Annie Tallon and Smith's stepfather were both given permission by the governor of the prison to remain in the

THE EAST HULL MURDER.

LAW TAKES ITS COURSE.

CONDEMNED MAN EXECUTED.

THIS MORNING'S SCENES OUTSIDE HULL GAOL.

Newspaper headlines indicating that William George Smith finally went to his death. Hull Times

prison's waiting room while the execution took place. His mother wanted to say a last goodbye to her son but that was not permitted.

As the hymns rang out, including *Nearer my God to thee*, many were overcome with grief, including one woman, later identified as a relative of Smith, who was inconsolable. As the minutes passed every man and boy in the crowd bared his head and the men stopped smoking. At two minutes to nine o'clock a few strokes of the bell inside the prison could be heard.

One feature of the death was the amount of media attention which followed it. Several cinematographs took views from the opposite embankment and close up of the prison, whilst there were also crowds of newspaper reporters who had travelled to the city from London.

The Home Secretary, Sir William Joynson-Hicks, said he was saddened by the death, despite having refused the appeal. He said that no fresh evidence on the case and no fresh consideration had been placed before him which would warrant him altering the decision of the judge and jury.

The papers gave their own final words on the death of George William Smith. The *Yorkshire Post* said:

> *Smith was guilty of an act of unjustifiable homicide, and by the law of the land has forfeited his own life. Neither the jury, including two women, nor the judge saw any reason to recommend him for mercy. The only reason for granting a reprieve would seem to be popular clamour. The inevitability with which a petition for reprieve seems now to follow any sensational murder points to a perversion of public sentiment which causes more sympathy to be extended to a murderer than to his blameless and unfortunate victim.*

The *Daily Dispatch* added:

> *Her death has deprived three children of their only protectress and had left them scarred with a hideous memory for life. By itself we cannot see how the case after being disposed of by British judge and jury (who gave no recommendation to mercy) could have aroused turbulent feelings afterwards.*

CHAPTER 3

Ripper Suspect with a Hull Connection 1891

As soon as his gruesome preparations were complete he sent for Marie and the children.

What do Jack the Ripper and Hull have in common? Maybe nothing, though there is an obvious connection in the shape of one man, Frederick Bailey Deeming, one of the nineteenth century's most notorious killers.

Deeming was executed in Melbourne, Australia and his most notorious murders occurred in Liverpool, however he had a strong Hull connection and was also a suspect in the Jack the Ripper investigations.

Deeming was born in Birkenhead near Liverpool around 1850, the youngest of seven children. He had what could be termed a troubled childhood, suffering beatings at the hands of his father who later died insane in a workhouse. His mother was a Sunday school teacher and she force-fed him her views of the Bible, leading him to have an obsession with the concepts of sin and punishment. He was devastated by her subsequent death and was to suffer a nervous breakdown. He later claimed that it was her spirit which compelled him to kill.

By 1890 he had, to some extent, grown out of his troubled childhood and was quite a handsome man who also had a well-practised way with words. He was able to convince others, notably young women, that he was a gentleman of aristocratic birth.

By the late 1880s Deeming had emigrated to Australia and was living there with his first wife, Marie, and

Frederick Bailey Deeming. Author's collection

their children. He was already no stranger to crime having been convicted of larceny, and during 1887 he appeared before a court in Sydney on bankruptcy charges and was sentenced to fourteen days imprisonment for failing to cooperate with the court. He hid large amounts of money from his creditors and set fire to his workshop to try and receive the insurance money. When that failed, and with the police on his tail once more, he absconded, firstly to South Africa and then on to England.

He first surfaced in Hull in October 1889 as an apparently wealthy man who went by the name of Lawson. He said that he was over from Australia and that he was a sheep and cattle rancher. A well dressed man with a love of fine clothes, who enjoyed staying in the best hotels, Lawson mixed largely with Hull and Beverley traders and stood out somewhat in the rough working class fishing port that Hull had become by the nineteenth century.

Deeming, or Lawson, met a young lady from Beverley called Nellie Matheson who lived with her mother and sister. Lawson used his well-used charm to move into her home and in 1890 the couple married at St Mary's Church in Beverley.

Some local people had already expressed some concerns about the new man in their midst and these were amplified when they learned that he made regular trips to Market Weighton to collect his post. However, the Matheson family were unaware of the rumours circulating around Beverley and the wedding went ahead. The honeymoon though, did not.

The Royal Station Hotel *where Deeming went on honeymoon with Nellie Matheson.* The author

Market place in Hull. One of Deeming's haunts. Author's collection

Lawson and Nellie arrived at the *Royal Station Hotel* in Hull for a short stay, but Lawson left, ostensibly on business, promising his new bride that he would be back before she knew it. She never saw him again.

Whilst in Hull his criminal activities had continued and he had bought large amounts of jewellery from Reynoldson in Whitefriargate, by cheque. Giving the shop his usual patter about his wealth, courtesy of the ranches of Australia, he was given the goods, but naturally the cheque bounced and the police were called in.

However, by the time they were on his tail, he had left the country. He left Hull for Southampton and there, boarded the SS *Coleridge*, bound for South America. When a distressed Nellie arrived back in Beverley after waiting for Lawson in Hull, there was a woman waiting to add to her grief. She introduced herself as Marie or Mrs Frederick Deeming from Birkenhead and said that her 'husband' was also known as Lawson. He had apparently telephoned his wife in Birkenhead and told her about his 'marriage' to Nellie. He also said that if the police arrived asking questions, to deny being married to him. On hearing this she decided to travel to Beverley and meet the woman also claiming to be married to Deeming/Lawson.

The women contacted Hull Police and Detective Sergeant Grassby dealt with the case which was ongoing after he received the information from Reynoldson jewellers. He found out that Lawson was aboard the *Coleridge* and ordered the ship to be stopped at the first available port, which turned out to be Montevideo in Uruguay. Police went on board and arrested Lawson who was taken into custody. The Hull fraud charges were used as the reason for arrest as no extradition treaty existed with Uruguay for bigamy.

Lawson was eventually sentenced to nine months inprisonment, serving his sentence at Hull's Hedon Road Gaol, before being released from custody in July 1891. However, during his time in prison he spent his time plotting the downfall of Marie, his first wife. He had abandoned family in Australia and the South Africa but both times Marie had tracked him down as she did when he was in Beverley. She had used her knowledge of his life of crime to blackmail him and demand that he support her and their four children, something he was desperate to avoid.

Lawson/Deeming arrived in Rainhill, a small town near Liverpool, later in July 1891 after his release from prison. He was now known as Albert Oliver Williams and told locals that he was a military officer home on leave from India. He leased Dinham Villa from a Mrs Mather saying that he was acting on behalf of a Colonel Brooks who would soon arrive from India to take up residence.

He told Mrs Mather that he was intending to stay for some time and somehow convinced her that the floors needed cementing. Unbeknown to her, he spent days digging a grave and packing the earth into travel trunks to dispose of. As soon

Hedon Road Gaol, Hull. The author

as his gruesome preparations were complete he sent for Marie and the children.

Early in August 1891 he killed them using an Australian battle-axe to knock them unconscious before cutting their throats. Neighbours later claimed to hear shrieks of terror which was probably the sound of the three elder children being killed when Marie was out with her baby. When they returned home, Deeming was waiting for them, knocking his wife down and slashing the baby's throat whilst it was still in Marie's arms.

It was later claimed that the children were exhumed wearing night-clothes so he could conceivably have killed them whilst they slept. He buried their bodies in the concrete and spent all night mopping up blood and destroying incriminating evidence. He even hired a cleaner to thoroughly scrub the house, to make sure there wasn't a trace of his family having been there.

Before leaving Rainhill, Deeming used his charm to entice one more woman into his web. He met and befriended Emily Mathers, a twenty-seven-year-old local girl. Saying he was a bachelor, she believed him, they began dating and they married in September. However, they were not to settle on Merseyside as Deeming already had plans for his new bride. He told neighbours that he was resuming his military duties in India and the couple sailed off on the SS *Kaiser Wilhelm II*. However, they arrived, not in India, but in Victoria, Australia and he settled Emily down in a town called Windsor, secretly making plans to kill her.

Deeming, still known as Albert Williams at this time, then bought cement, tools and a pan from an ironmongers in the town and, having all the ingredients for the murder, he proceeded with the grisly task, probably on Christmas Day 1891. Once again, he left the murder scene, first for Melbourne and then Sydney, no doubt checking the newspapers to see if the body of his wife had been discovered.

In fact Emily's body was not found until March 1892 when the new owner of the house was showing a prospective tenant round the property. He noticed a distinctly unpleasant smell coming from the bedroom and notified his estate agent. After investigating the fireplace the two men decided to call in the police and Deeming's plans were beginning to unravel. Police came to the house that day and spent about two hours digging through the concrete where they eventually discovered the entombed body of Emily.

The body was in an advanced state of decomposition and during the process of removing the body, the hair had become detached from the head. Eventually the police were able to get the body out and remove it to the local mortuary.

Police investigations led them to find that the last people to live in the property were a Mr and Mrs Drewin though they were soon to discover that they were also known as Albert and Emily Williams. They then identified Drewin as the man who had bought tools and cement from an ironmongers at around the time of the murder.

Police in Victoria subsequently learnt that Drewin had several aliases including Williams, and burnt papers in the fireplace in the Windsor flat further led police to believe that the couple had recently arrived in Australia from sea. On eventually learning that the man in question was actually known as Frederick Bailey Deeming, the Australian police contacted their colleagues in England whose officers were instructed to make a search of a property in Rainhill, Merseyside. To their horror they soon made the gruesome discovery of the bodies of Marie and the couples' four children under the fireplace of the villa Deeming had rented in Rainhill.

By this time Deeming was living in Sydney under the new alias of Baron Swanson and there he met his next intended

Artist's impression of the murder scene. Author's collection

prey. Kate Rousefell fell under his spell and the two arranged to marry. He told her that he would find work in Western Australia and that she would then follow him from Sydney and they would marry.

Though she did not know it at the time, Kate Rousefell had a lucky escape. The police undoubtedly saved her life when they stopped her in Melbourne whilst on her way to follow Deeming to Western Australia. The net was tightening around Deeming and the police eventually caught up with him in the town of Southern Cross in March 1892. He was returned to Melbourne and, following the inquest into the death of Emily Mathers, he was charged with her wilful murder and ordered to stand trial.

His arrest in Australia also had a link with Hull as it owed a little to Harry Webster, the Governor of Hull Prison. Webster had retired to Australia after leaving his job at Hedon Road on health grounds. He was in Melbourne and was reading a newspaper about a murder in the city and was particularly interested in the description of the man in custody.

He was also struck by the similarities between this murder and the Rainhill case which had been publicised prior to him leaving England. He went to see the Chief Constable of Melbourne who identified the man in custody as Lawson, who had been in prison in Hull for nine months. This set in process the task of linking all the crimes back to one man, Frederick Bailey Deeming.

Deeming's idea of burying his victims in concrete came from his time as an apprentice plumber. One of the places he worked was Chester Cathedral and his experiences there included penetrating the sepulchre as well as resealing the tomb in cement.

His carefully thought out plan worked well on Merseyside as there was the right soil, however in Australia the soil was more rocky and a combination of badly mixed cement and a hastily dug grave which was too shallow resulted in the awful smell seeping out of the flat and led, directly to his downfall.

Deeming's arrest aroused great interest both in Britain and Australia and the Melbourne courtroom was packed with many unable to get in to see the man described as a 'monster' in the press. Surprisingly with so many aliases and heinous crimes in both countries, the trial only took four days. Deeming made a desperate plea of insanity but the jury quickly rejected this defence and he was found guilty with the judge ordering him to be hanged.

Marshall Lyle, Deeming's solicitor, continued to plead on his behalf after the sentence, applying to the Privy Council for leniency on the grounds of his client's insanity, but his application was rejected and Deeming, or Lord Swanson as he still insisted on being called, was doomed. During the last few weeks of his life in the condemned cell at Melbourne Gaol he wrote his autobiography, recalling his life of crime in great detail.

Throughout 1892, as more was heard of Deeming, links were inevitably made between him and the Whitechapel murders in London. One paper even named him 'The Jack the Ripper of the Southern Seas'. It was a label which stuck and much press coverage centred on whether or not Deeming was the man who had been terrorising the prostitutes of London.

Many papers alleged that he had a friendship with Catherine Eddowes who was one of the Ripper's victims and one paper claimed that a London dressmaker had spotted Deeming in the east end of London on the night one of the Ripper murders took place. Another woman claimed to have had a long conversation with a man matching Deeming's description the day after Eddowes had been killed. The witness said that the man appeared to have a detailed knowledge of the crime, despite it only taking place the previous night.

To add fuel to the fire, Deeming spoke of his contempt for prostitutes in conversations with doctors in Melbourne Gaol who had been sent there to determine his sanity. He said to one that he had gone looking for a prostitute who had given him syphilis with the intention of killing her. He added, 'I've had my own back anyhow, as more than one of them has found out'. He also said that he believed in the extermination of all women.

Deeming himself kept a diplomatic silence on the rumours linking him with the Ripper murders, though one suspects he would have enjoyed the notoriety. One rhyme of the day went…

On the twenty-first of May,
Frederick Deeming passed away;
On the scaffold he did say –
'Ta-ra-da-boom-di-ay!'
'Ta-ra-da-boom-di-ay!'
This is a happy holiday,
An East End holiday,
The Ripper's gone away.

Deeming had maintained his calm exterior all the way to the gallows. Twelve thousand people ensured that the area around Melbourne Gaol was packed to the rafters, waiting patiently to receive confirmation that the killer was finally dead.

He was asked by the sheriff if he had any final words and shouted out 'Lord receive my spirit', seconds later the executioner pulled the lever and Deeming, noose around his neck, fell to his death. His body was removed after about an hour and, before burial, a death mask was made. This was sent onto Scotland Yard in London for help in the Rainhill case and in case the rumours about him being Jack the Ripper turned out to be true.

Deeming's body was eventually buried within the prison grounds before renovations, comparatively recently, led to the coffin being re-buried at Pentridge Prison.

Though it was natural that there would be speculation about Deeming being Jack the Ripper, it is unlikely that he was, despite him no doubt revelling in the notoriety it brought. The Whitechapel murders were limited to a concentrated area and were all prostitutes whereas Deeming's murders were people close to him, family members.

Also, the style of killing was different. The Whitechapel killer did not try and hide his victims. He mutilated them and then ran off before being caught. Deeming, by contrast, had obviously planned his murders systematically and made great effort to make sure that the bodies were never found. He had a motive for his killings, however grotesque whereas the Ripper did not. Still, despite being very unlikely, Deeming, during his time in England, could conceivably have been Jack the Ripper. We shall never know.

CHAPTER 4

Murder on the Farm
1903

Suddenly, the body of Annie Marshall came to the surface.

Close to the River Derwent, Scampston is a tiny rural hamlet in the heart of a prosperous area rich in agriculture, close to the border between the east and north ridings of Yorkshire. The nearest village of any size is Rillington which itself is five miles from the town of Malton. At the beginning of the twentieth century Rillington consisted of a few houses, five pubs, a fried fish shop and a railway station which often saw trains rattling through on the line between Hull and Scarborough.

However, few of the trains stopped at Rillington and such was the lack of demand that at Hull's Paragon Station the ticket office clerk wrote out tickets to Rillington in ink.

In 1900 Charles Ashton was employed as a farm labourer by George Brewster of Grange Farm near Scampston. Aged twenty, he was one of four farm hands working there. One of eight children from a poor family in Cottingham, Ashton was a typical farm servant with fair hair, broadly built and brawny; and a robust, ruddy complexion.

Brewster and others saw him at the farm as being a model employee, being

Annie Marshall. Hull Times

generally well behaved, with a good nature, though he occasionally displayed a quick temper.

One of the other people working at Grange Farm was Annie Marshall. Aged just fifteen she was employed as a servant. A short girl with delicate features, she was also popular on the farm and had a strong connection with the Brewster family. Annie had previously worked for Brewster and his wife at another farm they owned before they moved to Scampston.

Ashton and Marshall became good friends though there was never any hint of romance between them. She used to walk down to the village from the farm with a number of the farm hands and it was common knowledge that she was going out with a man called Sawdon whilst Ashton himself was dating a young girl. The two couples were often seen out together and were referred to by one person as the 'best of butties' (a local expression with the same meaning as buddies).

Marshall's parents lived in Lissett near Driffield and she wrote to them on Saturday, 19 September 1903. Through her writing, her parents could read that she was happy both in her work and in her personal life and they were looking forward to seeing her soon.

On Sunday, 20 September, Annie left the farm between five and half past five to go to church in Scampston. After the service she met up with a friend, Ada Pickering, and the two of them walked into Scampston village where they saw Ashton at about seven-thirty in the evening.

The three of them continued walking together until they reached the cricket field gate when Annie left them to continue home. Ashton walked with Pickering until they reached the railway gate, about half an hour from her home, where he left her to walk the rest of the way alone.

About an hour later, at nine o'clock, Ashton was recognised by two separate people when he was seen to be lying on the ground alongside a girl. A waggoner at the Stevenson farm, which was near to Grange Farm, was out with a young woman on the Sunday night, walking on the road towards Grange Farm when they came across another man and woman.

In the darkness a voice said 'good night' to the couple. It was already dark and when they passed, the man said, 'I will see who that is.' He was about to strike a match when the man on the ground said, 'Goodnight wag.' Recognising the voice of Ashton, the waggoner replied, 'Goodnight third.' The waggoner did not think anything of the incident and went on his way. He saw the form of somebody sitting or lying next to Ashton, but in the darkness did not know who it was.

Staff at Grange Farm waited up for Annie who was due back in at nine o'clock on the Sunday night, at about the same time as Ashton. Staff had heard some noises earlier in the night, some shouts and possibly even a gun being fired, but they did not link it in with Annie's disappearance. Ashton eventually turned up at ten thirty, but he was on his own and people at the farm began to become increasingly anxious for her welfare. They asked Ashton where she was but he merely replied that he had not seen her since earlier that evening and went to bed.

The only person who said that he had heard some shots was Hazlewood Brewster, George's son who had returned home at about half past nine that night. He said that the shots were fired one after another quite quickly and as far as he could tell, they came from the direction of the barley field at his father's farm.

He was not far from the shots when they were fired, but, suspecting that they were poachers and fearing for his own safety, he did not go any further to try and find out who was responsible.

Annie Marshall did not return home that night and George Brewster became involved the following morning, asking Ashton directly if he had seen the girl. Ashton replied, 'Yes, I have seen her against the cricket field gate and accompanied her to the railway gate.' Brewster then called the police who once again asked Ashton if he knew where she was. He gave the same reply but changed his story slightly, adding that he had heard two shots and seen some poachers, whilst he heard a cry like a hare though he said it could have been a child. He said it sounded like it was coming from the oatfield.

PC Broughton, an officer based at Rillington, had received the call on the Monday morning saying that the girl was missing. He was one of the officers who arrived at the farm and he searched around the area that day but found no trace. However, his suspicions of Ashton were first aroused when

Ashton re-told him the story of how he had followed some poachers and that he had heard a gun being fired and the sound of a hare being shot on the Sunday night. The police officer thought it unlikely that a poacher would fire at a hare in the pitch dark. He could not see the logic as the poacher would obviously not be able to see what he was aiming at.

Other officers organised a search party which was out all day on the Monday but they failed to find any trace of Annie, whilst PC Broughton searched the farm itself but returned home empty handed and said:

> *I went to bed but I could get no rest thinking of the affair. With the belief that it was to be solved around Brewster's farm I was up very early and down there again.*

On the Tuesday morning when Ashton and his fellow workers were carting corn, Ashton went into the stack yard carrying a hat which looked wet and bedraggled. He said, 'Here's Annie's hat, I have found it in the wheatfield.'

He showed it to Broughton when he returned to the farm on the Tuesday morning, and this served to increase the officer's suspicions of Ashton even further. He asked himself why was Annie's hat soaking wet when the weather in recent days had been warm and dry?

Broughton now firmly believed that Ashton knew more than he was letting on. However, he kept his suspicions to himself and they went on their way with the officer asking Ashton to take him to where he had heard the shots being fired. They found nothing to suggest that poaching had taken place and continued on their way.

PC Broughton. Hull Times

Ashton was talkative until they reached Scampston Beck, near to where, he claimed the hat was found. He pointed out to the officer a place under the fence where he said he found the hat and said to him:

> *My opinion is that someone has killed her and whoever did so has carried her to the black bridge and thrown her into the river or Scampston Beck.*

They went to the river and Ashton pointed to something in the water saying, 'There she is.' However, it was just a log of wood. He replied, 'Well, she won't be far from here. She will be between here and the bridge.' The two men walked further up the river before Ashton again stopped and cried out, 'Here's poor Annie', pointing to something in the water. The officer replied, 'No that's not a body, it's only a carpet bag', but Ashton continued, 'Why don't you see her leg?' Broughton then picked up a branch and pushed away some of the reeds on the riverbank. Suddenly the body of Annie Marshall came to the surface.

He blew his whistle and several farmers and their men abandoned the harvesting in a nearby field to assist the men in removing the body from the water and onto the riverbank. Ashton began crying, but Broughton nevertheless felt that he was a threat and ordered him to remove his coat. Once the body was out of the water, the officer noticed on her cheek, two bullet wounds and also saw that her mouth had been filled with tufts of grass.

The medical staff who were soon on hand said that there were two bullet wounds in the cheek, close together, having clearly been shot at close range as the flesh was scorched. Tracking the course of the bullet, they said that the bone at the base of the skull had been fractured which was itself sufficient to have caused death. A frothy mucus also came from her nose and mouth indicating that the lungs had some air in them when the body went into the water. Dr Adams examined the body and said that death was caused by gun wounds to the head.

PC Broughton went back to search the barley field and

found some artificial flowers strewn about forty yards from where Ashton said he found the hat. He also found a newly dug hole in the ground. Raking it out he found some more of the flowers and noted that the hole was certainly large enough to hold the hat.

He also found some blood on the side of the field path and signs of a violent struggle as the grass had been torn up and the ground was very cut up in places. The place where the waggoner had seen Ashton with a girl was also examined, which was where some other bloodstains were found.

The officer quickly cleared up the mystery of whether the body of Annie Marshall was dragged to the river bank or whether the murder took place where the body was found. Searching the fields near to the farmhouse he came across a patch of darkened blood in a field of barley stubble. It was here where the girl received the two fatal bullet wounds and there were a number of footmarks in the soft soil, indicating that a desperate struggle between the girl and her attacker had taken place.

The spot where the murder took place was within sight of the farm, which could be seen, with its windows partly hidden behind the rich foliage. Broughton gradually began to piece together the events of the Sunday night and estimated that at about nine thirty at night the murderer lifted the body of the girl on the edge of the barley field, carried it across an open meadow, shielded by the darkness. He then placed it in a dark corner behind some hedges where the hat was later found. He believed that the killer then returned to the body, picked it up, carried it to the river nearby and deposited it amongst the thick reeds.

PC Broughton was in no doubt that Ashton was the killer and arrested him on suspicion of causing the death. Ashton 'promptly and bitterly' denied the charge, but was handcuffed and taken to the nearest police station. He was remanded at Malton police court before being taken to Paragon Station en route to Hull Gaol. He was subsequently placed on remand at Norton police station and his presence caused quite a commotion in the immediate area with very few murders having taken place in the East Riding.

Paragon Station, largely unchanged since the early 1900s. The author

The night after Ashton's arrest, Broughton returned to the farm to conduct a further search and found a box in Ashton's bedroom. In it he discovered a six-chambered revolver, two small handkerchiefs and three unexploded cartridges in a jacket pocket. The revolver was unloaded but there was another case full of empty cartridges. On his vest were several small spots of blood and some trousers found in his room were also dirty with bloodstains on one of the knees.

The police also gained possession of the boots that Ashton wore on the Sunday night. They were covered with mud that could not have been picked up on the dry roads of that evening, leading to a belief that the mud was picked up on the river bank.

Meanwhile, in his prison cell, Ashton was coming to terms with his arrest. On the night after he was arrested, Sergeant Waind went into Ashton's cell to see that he was okay. He was lying on the bed shivering and, on being asked if he was warm enough he said, 'Come here, I want to tell you all.' He said to the officer, 'Do you think I shall get over it all right?' He admitted that he killed the girl but maintained that he never intended it to happen.

He told the sergeant:

First thing I was coming down the road. I did shoot at the girl. I don't know what I shot at her for. I took the policeman to the wrong box up my stairs. I dare not take him to my own. My own box is locked up. The revolver is in my jacket pocket and there are some cartridges in a box in the locker. I never did intend shooting the girl. Have you seen the girl? She looks a queer sight doesn't she?

Poor Annie! I wish I had not done ought at her. We were always such good mates me and the girl. I don't know how it was that night, it seemed to go wrong. Poor lass. I wish I'll never done nought at her. I've never had an hour's sleep since Sunday night. I seem as though I could nor rest without her. I took the girl to the river and where we found her I threw her in. I thought she would go away.

Luke White MP, the coroner, decided to hold the inquest into Annie Marshall's death at Grange Farm and Ashton was brought from Norton police station to be present. In every village en route crowds gathered to catch a glimpse of the prisoner and many other people crowded round the farm entrance to see him as he arrived.

Murders in this part of East Yorkshire were so rare that Luke White had not presided over a murder case in his seven years of office. The *Hull Daily Mail* saw this as a tribute to the immunity of the East Riding from serious crime as the last murder in the area had taken place twenty-eight years before.

Deciding that the rooms inside the farm were too small to accommodate the number of witnesses and jury, White decided to hold the inquest on the lawn outside. It heard from Hazelwood Brewster, the son of George Brewster, who said that he had heard a shot, followed by a scream and thought it must have been a hare. He also heard a second shot immediately afterwards.

PC Broughton, giving evidence, told the inquest that when searching with Ashton on the Tuesday morning, Ashton had said that in his opinion Marshall had been killed, carried to the river and thrown over the black bridge.

Dr Adams, who had examined the body, told the inquest that

Entrance to the inside of Hull Gaol. Hull Local Studies Library

he had found two bullets in the back of the head, one of which had fractured the skull. Death had been due to bullet wounds and suffocation. The post-mortem also revealed that Annie Marshall had been sexually assaulted and the body appeared to have been attacked. He said that Ashton was examined after his arrest and on his right hand were found marks, which corresponded to teeth bites.

At the inquest the jury returned a verdict of wilful murder against Ashton and he was committed for trial at York.

Though initially remanded from Norton court, there were no facilities in Malton or Norton to keep long-term prisoners so he was sent to Hull gaol for the remainder of his time in custody.

However, he had to return to Norton for formal committal several days later and, as he could see from the train window, the excitement in the case was still intense. Crowds gathered to see the train go past and the journey was completed with drawn blinds. When Ashton made his way inside, the crowded bench of magistrates at Norton finally committed the prisoner for trial.

Annie's parents were anxious to get her daughter's body returned and buried in the village where she was born. From a poor family, she was grateful that she would only have to pay half the expense as Brewster, in a goodwill gesture, arranged to take the body in a wagon halfway to her eventual resting-place. He took charge of the funeral cortège to Weaverthorpe and then the girl's friends brought it onto Lissett. On the morning after the inquest, the body of Annie Marshall was finally buried in Lissett. Many people from the local area joined the family of the deceased at the service.

Ashton's trial at York Assizes took place on 1 December 1903,

Map showing Lissett, where Marshall's parents lived. www.Mapquest.co.uk

where he reiterated his guilt saying, 'Yes sir, I did kill her but never intended.' His counsel said that in a sudden quarrel he shot the girl though he would not say what the quarrel was about.

Ashton's defence team asked the jury to consider reducing his charge to manslaughter, suggesting there was no clear motive or premeditation involved, but they were unsuccessful and he had to face trial for murder.

Hazelwood Brewster, the farm owner's son, giving evidence at the trial, said, once again, that he was afraid when he heard the shots being fired and thought it was poachers. He explained that he did not try to intervene as he was afraid for his own safety.

The judge turned on Brewster angrily, saying:

> *You ought to be ashamed, a hawking fellow like you to be afraid because you think there is something wrong. You are a disgrace to your landlord.*

On hearing all the evidence the jury reached a verdict promptly and found Ashton guilty of murder with a strong recommendation for mercy on account of his youth. Judge Grantham responded by saying, 'I wish I could find something to say on the prisoner's behalf. I have searched for an excuse but searched in vain.'

Despite the pleas for mercy, Ashton was sentenced to death. A petition was drawn up by Messrs Laverick, Son and Wray of

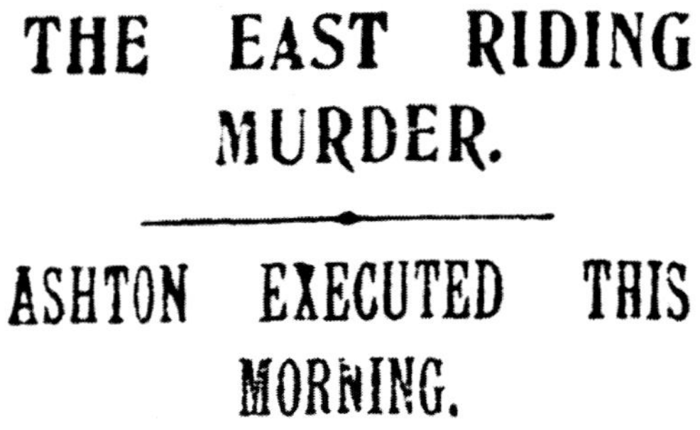
THE EAST RIDING MURDER.

ASHTON EXECUTED THIS MORNING.

Newspaper headline reporting that Charles Ashton had been executed. Hull Times

Hull, the solicitors who appeared for Ashton in court and about 2,000 signatures were gathered including that of Sir James Reckitt and a local MP, but the action did not have the desired effect and at just twenty years of age, Ashton was facing his last days in the condemned cell at Hedon Road Gaol.

Ashton was executed at nine o'clock on the Tuesday morning, 22 December 1903. About 300 people turned up outside the prison to witness the event and Ashton's body was interred in the prison grounds, in the same plot as that which carried the bodies of Arthur Richardson and William Bolton.

At the meeting of the Joint Standing Committee in January 1904, Charles Broughton, by now acting sergeant, was granted a merit badge with extra pay for the 'intelligence and promptitude he showed in dealing with the case'. The chairman of the committee said that had it not been for his tact, the murder may well have been unresolved.

As for the motive, Ashton took that to the grave. Colleagues of Ashton said after the trial that he had a quick temper and that he was jealous of Annie's blossoming friendship with another farm labourer from a neighbouring farm. It seemed, perhaps, the most likely explanation for the Scampston farm murder.

CHAPTER 5

Horrific Child Murder 1873

The constable went into the bedroom and was confronted with the sight of the body of Sarah Alice...

Thirty-year-old Jane Crompton lived with her husband John at 65 Osborne Street in Hull. The couple, who had lived there for about eight months, had been married for four years and had two children, Bertha Anne, aged three and Sarah Alice who was just a baby.

The apartment in Osborne Street was at the top of the house and was accessible by two narrow flights of stairs. It was poorly furnished although the couple tried to keep the apartment neat and tidy.

John worked as a baker for Stonehouse's in Chariot Street, a five-minute walk away from home, but was about to leave and undergo temporary employment elsewhere. Sarah Alice was just two months old in March 1873 and it was then that the Crompton's began to encounter one or two problems with the first cracks in their marriage beginning to appear. Jane especially was arguing with her husband constantly and

Part of Chariot Street today. The author

appeared very unsettled.

The problems appeared to be largely due to the poor relationship between mother and new daughter despite Sarah appearing to be a normal baby and not particularly fretful. Crompton had begun acting strangely and told neighbours that she could not do well for the child. She said that she had no breast milk and that the child had to be fed by a bottle.

Alice Fox, who lived next door to the Crompton's, was one of those most concerned that her next door neighbour had seemed to take a dislike to her own child. Crompton often asked Alice to dress the baby, saying, 'I'm very glad you've done that, I do not like the child.' She had also commented that if the child were in heaven what a good job it would be. However, Alice was reassured that John Crompton was a good husband, quiet, sober and hard-working and she felt sure that he would be a stabilising influence on his wife.

The problems between mother and new daughter had not improved by early May 1873 when Crompton, talking to Alice Fox, said, 'I shall do something to my baby, I cannot do anything with it.' Fox replied, 'If you do they will tickle you up for it.' Fox became more concerned for the welfare of the child and visited Crompton frequently to check on the baby. However, despite the warnings, she did not feel that Crompton would actually harm her own child, however unhappy she was feeling.

John left to go to work at about eight o'clock on the morning of 15 May 1873, kissing his wife goodbye. He had helped her with the children before leaving and she seemed in reasonably good health and spirits and was up and dressed with the baby on her knee and the eldest child getting her breakfast. John believed, perhaps more in hope than expectation, that his wife appeared to be becoming fonder of the child and went off to work, reasonably hopeful that the couple could work through their problems.

About half an hour later, Crompton went into the adjoining apartment, belonging to Alice Fox and said, 'Oh Mrs Fox, I've done something to baby.' Fox replied, 'Surely not.' Bertha, Crompton's other daughter, was with her and said to Fox, 'I watched mother take a key out of her pocket and unlock dada's box. She took the knife out and cut Alice's head off and laid it on the kilt' (she meant to say quilt).

Scarcely believing what she was hearing, Alice accompanied the mother and daughter back to their flat and was greeted by a quite horrendous sight. She saw the baby, partially dressed, lying in a pool of blood with the head completely severed from the body and lying about a foot away from it. The bedclothes were all over the room and were covered in blood.

Fox shrieked and ran downstairs where the landlady of the house confronted her, wondering what all the noise was about. Fox screamed back at Crompton, 'You wretch, you'll have to pay for murdering your baby.' She then grabbed her and pushed her out of the house. Crompton shouted, 'Oh, don't turn me over', but Fox said, 'You must go out, I have four children and how do I know you would not do something to them?'

PC Dixey, who was on duty in Osborne Street at the time, was called in to the house and could see that it was in a mess. The couple, especially John, had always been quite tidy despite having few possessions, but their domestic situation had clearly deteriorated in recent weeks and when the constable took a look around he saw that the place was unkempt. The breakfast things were still on the table and the bed in the corner of the room had not been made.

The constable went into the bedroom and was confronted with the sight of the body of Sarah Alice. Having made an initial check of the body, he believed that the mother took the knife and laid the face of the blade against the chin and cut the head off with the neck still being attached to the body.

A table knife, also covered in blood, was found in the bedroom. It was one of half a dozen knives that John had kept locked away in a box and was only used very occasionally. They had recently been sharpened, and that could be seen from the cut which removed the head, as it was not jagged in any way.

Crompton admitted the crime to PC Dixey but gave no reason why she did it and the news quickly spread around the neighbourhood that they had a murderer within their number. With police officers gathering inside and outside the apartment people came to see what all the commotion was about. When they heard the shocking news, anger built up and some tried to

Osborne Street, showing the only remaining early nineteenth century properties.
The author

attack Crompton, one woman rushing towards her with a knife in her hand. PC Dixey foiled the attack and managed to calm the situation down but he realised that he had to get her out of the house immediately and told her to get her bonnet and shawl on and go with him.

The constable took Crompton into custody and formally charged her with wilfully murdering her own child. She replied, 'Yes, I did it' and, having left Bertha with Alice Fox, went quietly to the police station.

Left behind, the people of Osborne Street did not know the full facts of the case so the rumour mill went into overdrive with many giving their interpretation on what happened inside the flat. One rumour went around that after Crompton mutilated Sarah Alice's body, she combed the hair on the baby's head and partly dressed the decapitated trunk before going into adjoining rooms to ask them to come and see how pretty the baby looked. It was also suspected that she was closer to Bertha as she wasn't her husband's child, but that of her former lover.

Once out of the house and en route to the police station, Dixey once again asked Crompton what she had done, trying to make some sense out of a horrific situation. She replied that she unlocked a box and took a new, sharp knife out of the half a dozen new knives that she had bought with the housekeeping she was given each week by her husband. When asked why she had done it, she said that she could never have done it if the two women who lived next door, meaning Alice Fox and a Mrs Wood, had not treated her as they did.

She asked PC Dixey if she would ever be forgiven to which he replied, 'I hope so.' She said, 'Do you think they will hang me?' He answered, 'I cannot say. I hope not.'

A large crowd of people besieged the house during the day after the murder with the case attracting a large amount of coverage in the neighbourhood and in the city at large.

The centre of Hull at the beginning of the twentieth century. Osborne Street is just off the bottom of the map. Hull Local Studies Library

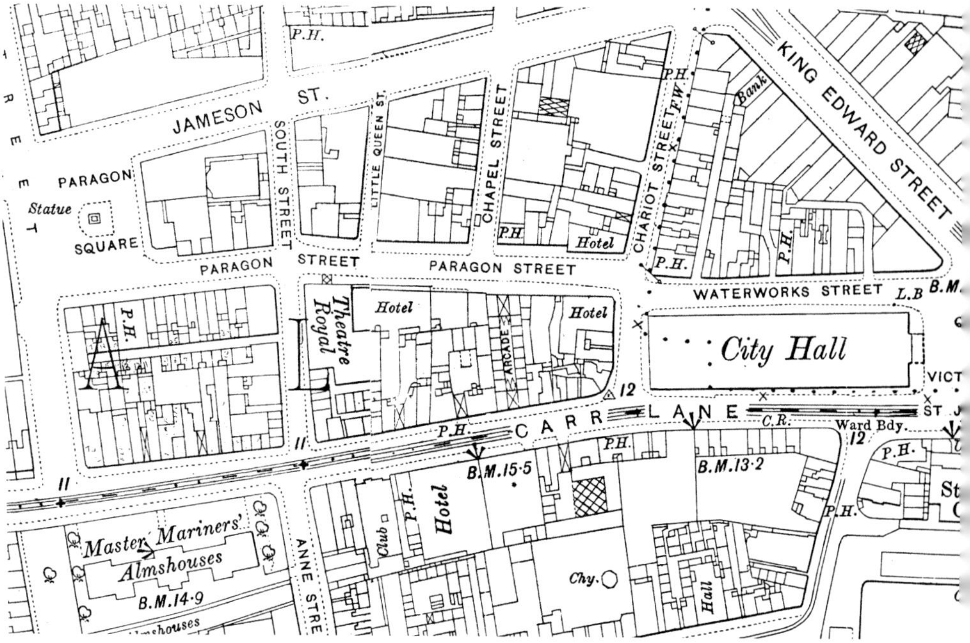

Meanwhile, Jane Crompton herself was in custody by this time. The day after the murder she was brought before the Hull Police Court where she was charged on remand before Mr Walter Wrangham for the wilful murder of her child, Sarah Alice. She again gave no reason for committing the crime apart from the fact that she had been in a depressed state of mind.

On the same evening, the inquest into the death of the baby was held at the *Tynemouth Castle* public house in Osborne Street before JJ Thorney, the coroner and fourteen jurymen.

John Crompton, still grieving the loss of his daughter, told the inquiry that his wife had been distressed in recent weeks and was concerned that she could not do much for the baby. She could not breast-feed and had to feed the baby with a bottle, though he stressed that the child was perfectly healthy.

Jane Crompton stared around the court vacantly during the time of her brief examination. She said very little, briefly praising her husband, saying that he was 'one of the best of men' and spoke of his kindness towards her and the children. She said that he was a steady, respectable man who brought home his wages, so poverty was not a reason for the crime having been committed.

In court, PC Dixey produced a large bright knife which, when he found it, appeared to have been wiped. He confirmed that this was the weapon used to commit the murder.

Alice Fox told the inquiry that in her opinion, Crompton did not bond with her new-born child very well, saying that she was often called upon to wash and nurse the child for which Crompton was grateful. She would say to Fox, 'I am so glad you have done it, I can't touch it. I shall never bring it up.' She frequently spoke to Alice Fox of how well she could do if she didn't have the baby and used to go to Fox's flat on several occasions saying how hard it was.

Fox used to become a little angry at this, saying that as she had four children compared to Crompton's two, she should not complain. However, Crompton used to reply, 'If only I could be like you, I could do my work but I can't. The child cries so.' Fox added that she would remember Sarah as a beautiful baby and not particularly fretful.

Crompton also used to say to Fox:

> *Do you think anybody who had no children of their own would take this? If so would give it them. I would take the other* [child] *and go away. We were very comfortable when we had no young baby.*

Fox found her behaviour very odd as she appeared to idolise her elder daughter, having a close relationship with her and appearing to be a good mother.

The coroner, in summing up, said that there was hardly any need for him to do so as the evidence all pointed towards the murder of the baby by its mother. He reminded the jury of what he had said at the outset. In respect of the woman's sanity, that was not an issue, it was only whether she had or had not killed the child. The jury therefore returned a verdict of wilful murder.

When asked if there was any reason why she should not be remanded in custody, she answered, 'No.' She was remanded for eight days and was taken to the borough jail where officials carefully watched her as she was considered to be quite a high suicide risk.

Jane Crompton was due to be tried at York Assizes on 5 June. She was said to be greatly distressed and told her counsel that she wanted to plead guilty to murder. However, when in court, the prosecuting barrister, Mr Lewis, said that the defendant had been in a depressed state of mind and had also had a deteriorating relationship with her husband. In response to this the judge asked her defence counsel if they could persuade her to change her plea as it may well be in her best interests. They eventually did so and she pleaded not guilty to murder.

Honourable Chandos Leigh, part of the defence counsel, in addressing the jury, said that from the state of the prisoner's mind at the time of the murder, she was not responsible for her actions as she had been suffering from melancholia, which had affected other members of her family.

Mr Tempest Anderson, deputy surgeon at York Castle, where she had been kept since her arrest, said that he had visited her on several occasions since she came to York. He agreed that she was suffering from melancholia and had many symptoms of

York Castle female prison. York Castle Museum

that condition. He added that the condition often led the sufferer to commit suicide or even murder. When she arrived at York Castle he ordered that she was not to be left alone as she continued to be quite a high suicide risk and he said that in conversations with her, she had said that her neighbours had annoyed her and put her 'out of love with her husband.' As a consequence, she had a feeling herself that something dreadful may happen.

He said that melancholia may lead to such a state of mind that the sufferer may not be aware of the action she was committing, or that she would not be able to stop any action she was committing. Anderson said that he was prepared to say that Jane Crompton was insane.

He had made enquiries in Hull and received a letter from a surgeon at a 'lunatic asylum' and found that Crompton had had numerous psychological problems. She also had a brother and cousin who were classed as insane and were incarcerated in the asylum. The surgeon said that in his dealings with her, she knew the difference between right and wrong, but probably didn't at the time the murder took place.

Captain Lowrie, the governor of York Castle, told the trial that he had also seen the prisoner frequently during her time in custody and that he too considered that her mind was affected. He said that since she entered prison she had been in a very nervous state and had been crying continuously.

The jury returned to court after a short time to consider the evidence and they returned a verdict of not guilty to murder on the grounds of insanity. Mr Baron Hollock said that the prisoner must be detained at her majesty's pleasure. No further mention of Jane Crompton could be found after this point, though it is unlikely that she ever tasted freedom again.

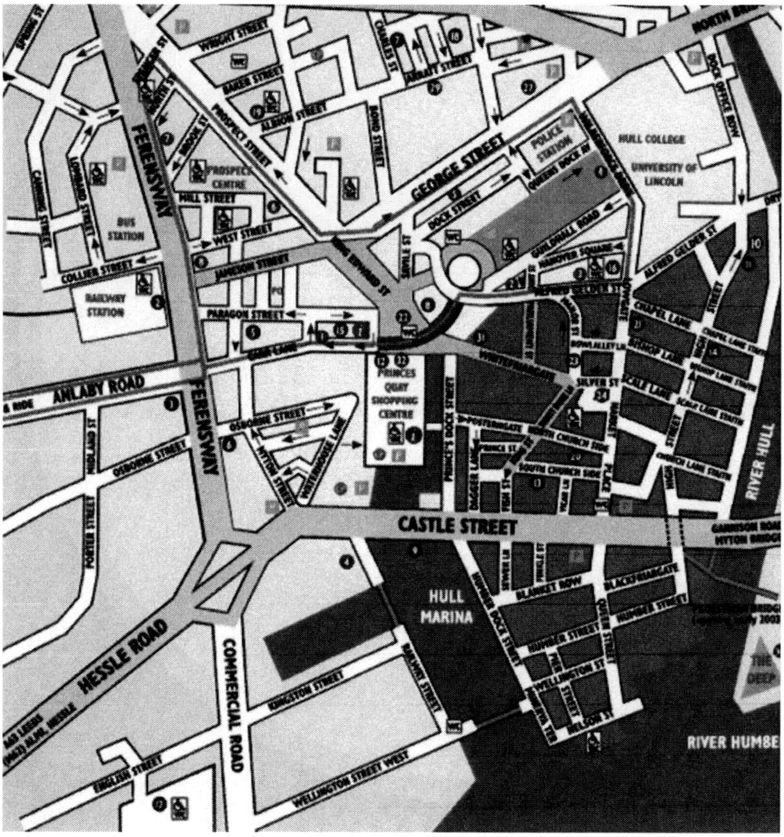

Hull city centre today. Hull City Council

CHAPTER 6

Murder within the Family
1901

He tried to account for the bloodstained clothing by saying that he had been involved in a fight...

Arthur Richardson was a Hull-born man with an unsettled start in life. He trained as a joiner but failed to find any firm willing to take him on, so in a bid to make a name for himself, he joined the army as a teenager and went out to India. However, that was also destined for failure as he was dismissed from the army and returned to Britain before getting married and, shortly afterwards, leaving his wife to settle in Brigg, Lincolnshire.

Richardson's life was threatening to come off the rails and an almost inevitable jail sentence came when he served six months in Lincoln Prison for robbing an aunt of £26. After his release from prison he crossed the Humber to Hull and lodged with a

Walker Street as it stands today. The author

Hodgson Street today. The author

couple called Skelton who lived in Faith Terrace, Walker Street. He told the Skelton's that he had found work at Reckitt's factory and duly left home every morning at about five o'clock, presumably to go to work. It fooled the Skelton's but Richardson did not have a job at Reckitt's or anywhere else. He had made the story up so that they would allow him to continue lodging with them.

Sarah Hebden was another of Richardson's aunts and, as a boy, Richardson frequently visited her house and knew her well. However, it appeared that Hebden was not especially pleased to see him when he reappeared in Hull after his spell in Lincoln. Being without work, Richardson needed money and he found his aunt an easy touch. He saw her out in east Hull shortly after he returned to the city and noticed that she appeared afraid of him, refusing to look him straight in the eyes.

Hebden lived at 97 Hodgson Street and she acted as an agent for the Royal Liver Friendly Society. On her weekly collections she took approximately £2 and she usually kept savings of about £10 in a tea caddy at her home.

On Thursday, 28 November 1901 she was due to visit friends in Elloughton but never arrived. Later in the day a girl called

Jackson, a friend of Hebden's went to her door but did not get an answer and went next door to the house of Margaret Bower, Sarah Hebden's sister, who was also Arthur Richardson's mother.

Bower and Jackson went to the offices of the Royal Liver Friendly Society but found that Hebden had not been there to take in the money, as she usually did. By the evening Margaret Bower was becoming increasingly anxious and sent her daughter, Florence Gertrude, to try and get into Hebden's house next door. She gained entrance through the back kitchen window and with a lighted candle in her hand shone the light through the entrance to the kitchen door. In the flickering light she could just make out her aunt's body lying on the floor.

The police were called and soon arrived at the house. There they found two large pools of blood at the scene, one close to the foot of the stairs at the entrance to the kitchen door and the other further along the passage leading to the door into the backyard. By the body were found a pair of tongs, which had been bent. A piece of the tongs which had been broken off in the attack was found under her body. Mrs Hebden had been battered to death, her head was a mass of bruises and one of her fingers was barely hanging onto her hand, while another was badly dislocated.

The police were told that hidden upstairs would be the tea caddy with her insurance book and two purses. They searched the house and underneath her bed was found the tea caddy, but it had been broken open, probably by the tongs. It contained two empty purses and a newspaper cutting relating to Richardson, reporting that he had been sentenced to six months in prison for the Brigg robbery.

At about half past seven on the Friday morning, Arthur Richardson was seen at the corner of Craven Street, Hedon Road, talking to an old friend. He told the man that he had money in his pocket and that he was 'living off the fat of the land' after a successful bet on a horse race.

Later that day he ordered a suit and an overcoat for which he gave a false name and address. Suspicions were raised amongst people who knew Richardson when they saw him in the new clothes as he had only been seen before in the same set of

Hedon Road today. The author

grubby working clothes. He told friends that his new look was to impress his estranged wife and that same night he went back to the Skelton's house brandishing a gold watch though he didn't offer an explanation of where it had come from.

When details of his aunt's death was in the papers, on the Friday afternoon, Richardson returned to his lodgings, apparently in grief. He claimed to have been told of her death by a work colleague at Reckitt's and later that day he was spotted in his local pub crying. However, despite his impression of a grieving nephew, the Hull police were on his tail. They knew of the robbery in Brigg and also knew, crucially, that Sarah Hebden was afraid of her nephew and did not trust him.

They finally caught up with Richardson on 30 November, two days after the murder and arrested him. His clothes were covered in blood and he had in his pocket, £10, thought likely to have been money taken from the tea caddy in the house. He admitted that the gold watch did belong to Sarah Hebden but said that she gave it to him to get the glass fastened. He tried to account for the bloodstained clothing by saying that he had been involved in a fight with a man in the Corporation Field on the day of his arrest.

Police believed that, leaving home on the morning of the murder, telling the Skelton's that he was off to work at

Arthur Richardson. Hull Packet

Reckitt's, he instead went straight to the home of his aunt who lived alone. It was not known how he got into the house, but he probably gained entrance through the back door whilst she was popping in and out of the house. After killing his aunt he took from the house the £10, the gold watch and a brooch.

At Hull police court before stipendiary magistrates, Richardson admitted telling the Skelton's he was working for Reckitt's, claiming that he lied about his work situation in order to assure them that they would receive his rent.

He told court, 'I really expected to get work there during the week and I told them I'd got it to make them feel sure they would get their money.' He said that he received the watch on the morning of Monday, 25th from his aunt in Bridge Street.

He said that he told his aunt that he would get the watch repaired and would give it to her when he next saw her. He

Staff of Reckitt & Sons in the early twentieth century. Author's collection

claimed that he found the brooch in Grimsby and said that his bloodstained clothes were in that state when he went into Lincoln prison, changing his story. He explained that he had a nosebleed when he first got to the prison and the blood trickled down onto his clothes and he had not washed them since. Richardson was remanded in custody and ordered to stand trial at the next York Assizes.

At his trial, Mr Kershaw, for the defence, said that a more probable hypothesis than that put forward by the prosecution was that some man, who perhaps knew Sarah Hebden's habits, concealed himself in the house the previous night. The following morning he followed her downstairs and killed her with one blow. The condition of the body when found was more in favour of the woman having been killed overnight or in the early morning.

Kershaw said he was aware that there were discrepancies in the story of Richardson but said that there were good reasons which would explain why he had not told the truth. He had said to his landlord that he was in work because of the stigma of being labelled a loafer if they had got to know that he was, in fact, out of work.

Kershaw said that whilst there may be suspicion hanging over the prisoner, he argued that it did not amount to sufficient to 'send him out of the world in the most ignominious way.' However, the barrister evidently had his own doubts about the effectiveness of Richardson's case as at one point he held up scraps of prison paper, full of holes and scribbled notes from Richardson and said this was the only evidence he had in pressing the case for the defence. The jury, including Sir James Reckitt, retired at five minutes to nine and had reached a guilty verdict just twenty minutes later at nine fifteen.

Asked if he wished to say anything, Richardson replied, 'All I have to say is that I am innocent and whatever punishment I receive is unjust.' Mr Justice Lawrence replied, 'Every fact in the case points in one direction, and that direction is your guilt.' He added that Sarah Hebden had been in fear for her life and did have a foreboding that Richardson would be responsible for her death. He then duly passed the death sentence on Richardson.

Paragon Station at the beginning of the twentieth century. Author's collection

The prisoner was brought back to Hull by train and he and the two prison warders were met by a small crowd of people back at Paragon Station. Richardson smiled as he stepped onto the platform before being escorted away into a cab towards Hedon Road prison.

An appeal against the death sentence was rejected by the Home Secretary, to the anger of Richardson's family who thought the evidence against him was largely circumstantial. They also said that Richardson's mind had taken several turns for the worst since leaving the army.

Richardson, meanwhile, continued to protest his innocence, even when the sentence of death had been passed. Whilst at Hedon Road gaol he was visited by his mother, his estranged wife and Mrs Ridgeway of the Salvation Army. He was also visited by the prison chaplain daily.

During his final days, Richardson was treated, as was customary, in a more generous way than the ordinary prisoners. He had certain privileges including food but was not allowed to associate with the other prisoners at exercise and even in chapel he had a pew specially screened off from other people where he would sit with two warders. One of his last acts was to finally admit his guilt and he wrote a statement revealing that he had murdered Sarah Hebden.

PRISON COMMISSION 26 MAR. 1902 H.O. REGISTRY RECEIVED MAR. 1902

A63235/17240. 17008/593

The following is the confession of Arthur Richardson which he desired me to make known to the, Lawful authorities.

'I, Arthur Richardson, did wilfully murder my Aunt Sarah Hebden, my motive in entering her house was not theft but murder. I trusted to chance to provide me with the weapon & took nothing with me for the purpose. I entered her house at 7.30 on the morning of the murder & I remained there an hour & a half, leaving about 9 o'clock making my escape across the Grover allotments. When I entered the house my Aunt & I had some words & in trying to avoid me, tripped over something & fell, in which attitude I struck her a blow, she then reached the tongs & knocked behind the fire grate to arouse the neighbours; I took the tongs from her &, struck her with them on the neck; she then arose & staggered towards the door behind which her body was found – whilst there & to silence her screams, for a knock at the door frightened me, I struck her with the tongs until she died. The most horrible part of the murder for me was some words my Aunt uttered just as she was dying; taking my hand in both hers she said, 'I forgive you all Arthur' & then died – At the same moment I heard a voice close behind me which said audibly, 'Murder will out'. it was the voice of my conscience'.

Signed J. W. Parkin.
Acting Chaplain.

March 25th 1902.

Forwarded
W R Chidley
Governor

HM Prison Hull

Written confession by Arthur Richardson whilst in prison. HM Prison, Hull

Richardson woke up at five o'clock on his final morning and managed to eat a hearty breakfast an hour later, despite the knowledge that he only had two hours left to live. Amongst his final visitors was the acting prison chaplain, the Reverend Parker and Richardson took his last Holy Communion.

Shortly before eight o'clock, William Billington, the executioner, arrived at the Hedon Road Gaol. They had met the previous evening with Billington making a special visit to meet Richardson in the condemned cell. Rather gruesomely, he was also, in effect, measuring up Richardson regarding his suitability for the gallows that he was preparing; as Richardson was of a slight build, he would need a longer rope than usual. It is not known whether the condemned man knew he was being 'measured up'! The scaffold on which Richardson was to hang was situated in the coachhouse at the prison.

A large crowd gathered outside the prison even though it was a wet and cold winter's day. People came from all parts of the city to witness the hoisting of the black flag and they began gathering as early as seven in the morning. The crowd was mostly made up of men, but there were also many women present, some of whom brought young children to witness the gruesome spectacle.

Silence grew as the hour of eight approached and a buzzer on the Alexandra Dock sounded to mark the hour. As Billington walked into the condemned cell, Richardson rose and held out his arms, allowing them to be pinioned.

When on the scaffold, he stood erect but just as Billington was about to move forward to begin the final preparations, Richardson fell to his knees and, speaking quietly, said, 'I confess my guilt and wish to go forth to my fellow men.' He then allowed his legs to be pinioned, the rope was fixed, the cap placed over his head and the bolt was pulled, all in a few seconds. Richardson disappeared from view and the rope merely gave a slight twitch, death apparently was instantaneous. The whole procedure, from leaving his cell to his death, took little more than a minute.

At that moment the ominous black flag came into view at the top of the prison and it fluttered gently in the breeze. A slight cheer could be heard by some in the crowd but it quickly faded

A63259/16

CERTIFICATE OF SURGEON.

31 *Vic.* *Cap* 24.

I, Edmund Henry Howlett the Surgeon of His Majesty's Prison of Kingston-upon-Hull hereby certify that I this day examined the Body of Arthur Richardson, on whom Judgment of Death was this day executed in the said Prison; and that on that Examination I found that the said Arthur Richardson was dead.

Dated this 25th *day of* March 1902

(Signature), [illegible]

No. 279

(7599)

Richardson's certificate of death. HM Prison, Hull

away as a more solemn and respectful mood prevailed. The crowd soon began to disperse although some remained in the vicinity of the prison for the whole time that the black flag was flying, which was about an hour.

Richardson's execution was the first occasion since 1778 that the death sentence had been carried out in Hull. Since that time prisoners from Hull who were to be executed had either been transported to Leeds or York.

York Castle conducted its last hanging in 1896 when August Carlson walked to the scaffold having been convicted of murdering his common law wife, Julia Wood, having cut her throat with a razor. However, when the castle was turned into a military prison, the county sheriff of York had to look elsewhere to carry out the death penalty.

Opened in 1870, the Hedon Road Gaol in Hull was the perfect solution for Hull murderers. The prison was the third to have been built in Hull and at the beginning of the twentieth century, the gallows at Hedon Road would see several notorious Hull murderers meet their end.

The actual gallows on which Richardson met his end were not built specifically for him but for twenty-one-year-old John Aaron Walker who murdered his father in Raywell Street in Hull but who was reprieved from the death sentence due to his youth, so Richardson had the dubious honour of being the first prisoner to be executed at Hedon Road.

Below: *The new Gaol in Castle Street, 1789.*
Hull Local Studies Library
Right: *The condemned cell at York Castle.*
The author

CHAPTER 7

Murder in Bog's Place
1901

Amos had been battered almost beyond recognition.

The year 1901 will go down in history of Hull as one of its most infamous with several murders occurring in the tough fishing port.

One such crime occurred in Bog's Place at the rear of some houses in West Street where access was gained by a short alley. The houses were two-roomed tenements which occupied one side of a yard, fifteen yards by twenty, which faced the back of the houses on the north side of West Street. The left of the yard was occupied by coalhouses whilst a blank wall was on the right-hand-side.

Alfred Fairfax, a fireman who worked aboard trawlers, lived in one of these tenements along with Norah Amos. Amos, aged thirty-two, had come to Hull after being transferred from Liverpool Prison to Hull Jail a few months earlier, having served a sentence for theft. Upon her release she decided to stay in Hull and she acquired several aliases, notably Norah, Annie and Daisy Bell. Of Irish ancestry and with a distinctive Irish/Scouse accent she had become known to many local people as 'Irish Biddy'.

The house in Bog's Place where the murder was committed. Hull Times

The relationship between Fairfax and Amos had not been happy for some time and arguments were common. Fairfax had just returned from a trip on a local trawler and the couple were drinking heavily, not for the first time.

On the evening of 13 June 1901, people heard the sound of the two of them having a blazing row. A couple of neighbours knocked on the door to try and intervene but each time they were left alone, the two would resume their fierce arguments and neighbours soon heard the sound of breaking furniture and the smashing of crockery. The fight between the couple had spilled over into the street and became so violent that the police were called. By eleven o'clock that night some semblance of order had been restored and the couple had been sent back indoors. The police were satisfied that the incident was under control and left to return to the station.

However, the quiet did not last long and another argument began shortly after the police had left. The noise levels rose and a neighbour called Howard went round to the house at about one o'clock in the morning. He told Fairfax, 'Let the woman alone and make less noise.' Fairfax replied, 'I won't. I'll put her out of mess before morning and I'll hang for her.' Sarah Norris, another neighbour of the couple heard them arguing and listened to Amos say to Fairfax, 'Oh Alf, you are a murderer.' Edward Sunman, landlord of their house, who lived nearby, said that when he went to his window to shout at them to stop rowing, he asked Amos what was the matter. She replied, 'He's calling me again.'

However, arguments between the pair were so common that the neighbours, although concerned, appeared to be of the belief that the couple would soon make up and return to normal.

At about eight o'clock the next morning, Edward Sunman went to the property to check on any damage that may have been caused during the argument between the couple. On opening the front door he found, to his horror, the body of Norah Amos lying in the corner of a room at the bottom of the stairs, naked with the exception of her stockings. She was badly bruised and the house was showing the damage caused by the rows with broken furniture and lots of smashed crockery. Some of these items were smeared with blood and it appeared that a terrible struggle had ensued. Amos had been battered almost beyond recognition.

Sunman assumed she was dead, but on closer examination he discovered she was still breathing, however it was very faint and he wasted no time in calling for an ambulance.

PC Shooter was on duty in nearby Paragon Street at about twenty past eight in the morning when he noticed a man, his clothes and boots covered in blood, coming towards him. It was Alfred Fairfax and he was approaching the constable with the intention of giving himself up.

He told the officer, 'I've murdered Biddy' and expanded on who Biddy was and what had actually happened. The constable accompanied Fairfax back to the house to see for himself whether the man's claims were true. He was suspicious, as Fairfax appeared to be suffering from the after-effects of drink and was still quite dazed, but back in Bog's Place they found Amos, still alive but deeply unconscious.

Dr McNidder arrived at the house, having been called by Sunman but his attempts to save her life were in vain and she died about fifteen minutes later. There were all the appearances of a prolonged and violent struggle. Initially the police thought that her attacker may have used a knife but later the police decided that a heavy weapon had been used in the attack.

PC Shooter and Fairfax were still in the house at this point but when the doctor pronounced Amos dead, Shooter formally

Paragon Street today. The author

arrested Fairfax on suspicion of causing her death. Sunman asked what the constable was doing and Shooter told him he was in custody because 'this man has given himself up for killing Biddy.' Sunman replied, 'Nonsense, the man is in the horrors of drink.' Fairfax said, 'It is no use Mr Sunman, I have murdered her. I thought it best to give myself up.'

Fairfax was charged with the wilful murder of Norah Amos and he appeared before the City Police Court on the Wednesday morning, clean and smart, having been provided with a blue dungaree jacket.

Fairfax was also present at the inquest into the death, held on the same day. After the jury had looked at the body of his former partner, he was taken to the coffin and looked at the face of the deceased, stooping to kiss her forehead twice and muttering 'Oh dear, oh dear.' He began to weep over the body and his grief seemed, to those present, to be genuine and spontaneous. The son of Amos, who had been on a training ship in Southampton, was also present and wept throughout the proceedings.

Dr McNidder, who had conducted a post-mortem on the body, told the inquest that there was not a fracture of the skull and all the wounds were consistent with kicks or blows. Death was due to exhaustion, following a great loss of blood. He added that no single wound would have resulted in her death though she undoubtedly died due to the combination of the wounds which were inflicted on her.

Dr Mike Mason, Medical Officer of Health also spoke of the post mortem and said that in his opinion she had been rendered insensible through the attack and concussion of the brain had set in. He thought that the blow on the head was the last one she received and stated that in his opinion the cause of death was a combination of concussion of the brain, shock, loss of blood and the result of extensive wounds.

He said that the wounds on the body may all have been caused by kicks with a boot belonging to Fairfax which had steel toeplates on, or by crockery being thrown at her.

Chas Goffin, a fisherman from Waterhouse Lane, also gave evidence to the inquest and said that he had known Norah Amos, who he knew as Mary Ann Amos for about eight years

SHOCKING MURDER IN HULL.

Woman's Terrible Death.

ARREST OF THE MURDERER.

Newspaper headlines reporting the murder of Norah Amos. Hull Times

and that he himself had lived with her for about five of those eight years. The two of them had lived in Yarmouth as well as Hull and he said that in his time with her, he never knew her as a drunk, she was always a well-behaved woman. He said that she had three children and one of them, Robert, often came to stay with her.

He added that he knew Fairfax as Hallman and the accused man admitted in court that Hallman was his father's name. Under cross-examination by Fairfax himself, Goffin admitted that he and the deceased woman had cohabited in the time that she had been with Fairfax, the most recent time being about six months before her murder.

Edward Sunman, the couple's landlord said that he had often heard them quarrelling and said that since Fairfax had returned from his work at sea he had heard 'Biddy' doing a lot of the shouting with her calling Fairfax names.

The Coroner told the inquest of the house at the time of the incident and said that every piece of furniture in the house was broken with the exception of a washing stand. Though the woman was nude when found, her clothes, when they were eventually discovered, had been torn to pieces.

He said that the woman had been terribly injured with many cuts and bruises and some of her teeth had been knocked out. He also said that some of the injuries had been inflicted with a blunt instrument, possibly a plate or a basin. Her arms were badly bruised, as it appeared she had made an attempt to protect herself and he estimated that the attack must have lasted quite a while.

Fairfax's subsequent trial at York Assizes did not focus on whether or not he had killed Norah Amos, which was not in doubt, rather the question for the jury was that if a person was drunk at the time he or she committed a crime, could the crime could be reduced from murder to manslaughter? The jury had to consider, whether they believed that Fairfax was in such a condition so as not to be able to form a deliberate intention. If that was the case, the judge argued, then they would be justified in delivering a verdict of not guilty of murder but guilty of manslaughter.

Harold Thomas, prosecuting, said that relations between Amos and Fairfax had become heated, with each of them addicted to drink and arguments became more frequent and increasingly violent.

Sarah Norris, who also lived in a house rented off Sunman, gave evidence and said that on the night of the attack, Fairfax and Amos were in the *Cauldron Cup* public house with Fairfax paying for her glass of beer. She said that about five o'clock on the Tuesday morning, she heard Amos say, 'You are a murderer, I'll have no more of it.' She added that Fairfax appeared to be very fond of Amos and that, though they were always arguing, she had become accustomed to it and it did not alarm her.

Louisa Kennedy, who lived in West Street, said that she heard Amos shout 'murder' and 'don't hurt me Alf' on the evening in question. At one o'clock on the Tuesday morning she looked out of her bedroom window and saw Fairfax and Amos in the yard. Fairfax knocked her down and kicked her on the body and Amos cried out, 'Don't hurt me Alf, I won't do it again.'

She then saw Amos being dragged out of the house twice and Fairfax warning that if she went out into the street she would be locked up, as she was drunk. Later on she alleged that Amos was trying to get out of the house but Fairfax wouldn't let her. Kennedy said that she heard the sound of Fairfax beating her and then saw, from the outlines through the window, Amos

West Street today. The author

being struck on the face before being thrown out of the front door. She heard the previous witness, Sarah Norris call out to him, 'You are a cowardly brute.'

PC Shooter told the trial that when interviewed, Fairfax appeared to be suffering from the effects of drink. He admitted that he had killed 'Biddy' in the house in West Street and that Shooter did not believe him at first but when they neared the house, Fairfax insisted, 'I think I have.' Shooter asked him what he had used for a weapon and Fairfax replied, 'With my fist.' Shooter produced at the inquest, a number of pieces of broken basin, which were covered in blood.

Mr Kershaw, in defence, pointed out the responsibility which rested with the jury. He was not going to say that the prisoner was not guilty, he argued that, upon the evidence, Fairfax was guilty of manslaughter rather than murder. He added that the couple were affectionate towards each other and said that when Fairfax committed the offence, owing to the influence of drink, he had ceased to be a thinking man and had become a wild beast. He said that there was no premeditation and that the incident occurred when the couple were in the middle of a drunken row and Fairfax was too heavily under the influence of alcohol to have truly know the consequences of his actions.

Summing up, the Lord Chief Justice pointed out the

difference between murder and manslaughter and added that drunkenness was no answer to the crime though it was an important element in it. He said that after the crime had been committed, the accused did not act like a man who had just committed wilful murder. He gave himself up to the police and when he returned to the house, he sat on the sofa and cried.

He said that the jury had to take these aspects of the case into consideration when they asked themselves the question of whether it was murder with forethought or 'a drunken affray in which one possibly fought the other.'

The jury retired and after an absence of only five minutes, they returned to deliver a unanimous verdict of manslaughter. The Lord Chief Justice, in passing sentence, said that the jury had taken a view of the case which he thought was justified by the facts. However, he strongly condemned Fairfax, saying that Amos had been kicked to death 'in a terribly violent manner' and said that she must have suffered fearfully.

He added, 'It was quite clear. It was due to the terrible curse of drink in which the prisoner had indulged and which had culminated in this crime.'

He said that the offence must be punished severely and he had no alternative but to pass a sentence of ten years' penal servitude.

Alfred Fairfax. Hull Times

CHAPTER 8

Moses in Daughter Murder
1901

...he fired two shots at point blank range and fled the scene, leaving his daughter bleeding to death.

Harry and Rosetta Forsey were a happy, newly married couple, setting out on a new life together. Everything appeared to be falling into place for them. They had set up home at 2 George's Terrace, St Mark Street in East Hull and were busy making plans for the future when their world took a completely unexpected and devastating turn.

Harry Forsey, a twenty-seven-year-old fireman worked at Reckitt's, a major employer in Hull as it remains. Rosetta, a year younger, didn't work as she practically had a full-time job in looking after her ailing mother. As their marriage plans took shape, there was only one cloud on the horizon. Moses Whitty, Rosetta's father was a labourer who had worked for the British Gas Company for the past nineteen years. A respectable man living in St Helena Gardens, Sculcoates Lane, Whitty, aged fifty, was bitterly opposed to the marriage and had even threatened to kill Harry if the wedding took place.

St Helena Gardens, where Moses Whitty lived. The author

Whitty's wife, Rosetta's mother, was an invalid and it was believed that his main objection to the marriage was that it would mean that Rosetta would be spending less time looking after her mother. So fierce had his objections been that shortly before the marriage, Rosetta left her parent's home and went to live with a cousin. His protests did not work however and Rosetta and Frank were married at St Paul's Church on St Paul's Street on Saturday, 23 March 1901. They chose this church as it was far enough from Whitty's house to ensure that he would not find out that the marriage had taken place. In fact it wasn't until the following Tuesday that Whitty had heard the news.

Despite the hostility that Whitty undoubtedly felt about his daughter's forthcoming marriage, he evidently did not want to lose contact with her as he had bought her and Harry, a clock, a sewing machine and a dressing table as wedding gifts, even though he never gave them to the happy couple.

On 29 March Rosetta took Harry's dinner to him at Reckitt's on Dansom Lane just before midday. She appeared to be cheerful, in good health and was looking forward to seeing her husband after work.

Below: *St Paul's Street, where the church used to stand.* The author

Left: *St Paul's Church.* Hull College Local Studies Unit

The 'Reckitt' factory as it is today. The author

Later that afternoon, at about four o'clock, Rosetta was finishing off her domestic duties, washing the dishes in her kitchen when there was a knock at the back door. Still with a wet saucer in her hand, she opened the door to be confronted by her father holding a gun pointing straight at her head. She let out a scream but he fired two shots at point blank range and fled the scene leaving his daughter bleeding to death.

Some residents heard the commotion. Jane Harrison lived in a house opposite Rosetta and at about four o'clock she heard a low scream followed by a much more violent sounding one. She was about to go into the house along with another neighbour, Elizabeth Bushby, when she saw a man strolling out of the house. Looking noticeably pale he was walking slowly away towards town. Having seen him before, she was sure it was Moses Whitty.

The two women could smell smoke and followed the smell to the rear of the house where it became stronger and smelt more like gunpowder. They went through the kitchen and eventually found Rosetta lying in the back yard in a pool of blood.

They raised an alarm and PC Clayfoot soon arrived. When he entered the house he found the woman lying on the floor with, as the *Hull News* later rather insensitively described it, 'her brains blown out'. He was told that a man had been seen leaving the house moments after the shot had been fired.

Dr Harold and Dr Townley arrived at the scene, though they could do nothing to aid Rosetta except confirm that she was dead, killed by two gunshot wounds to the head. Cause of death was due to shock caused by a haemorrhage of the brain and Dr Harold estimated that death would have been instantaneous.

Nicholson Street over a mile away from George's Terrace, was the home of Eliza and Frank Forsey, Rosetta's parents-in-law.

At about five-thirty on the same afternoon, Eliza was in the kitchen with her daughter, whilst her husband was unwell and upstairs in bed. There was a knock on the door and Eliza, upon answering it saw Moses Whitty on the doorstep. Though not an expected visitor she was not concerned as Whitty appeared calm and collected and though she knew his views on the marriage, she did not expect any unpleasantness.

Whitty held out in his left hand a letter and said, 'This is for Hetty' meaning his daughter, who he had killed only minutes before. Eliza took the letter from him and Whitty, who had kept his hand in his right pocket, suddenly drew the revolver and fired three shots at Eliza. One of the bullets lodged above the hip and she staggered into the back kitchen before falling to the

Nicholson Street today. The author

ground. Her daughter ran screaming into the street to try and get help.

Eliza recovered her feet and crouched under a table, while Eliza's husband Frank rushed downstairs, on hearing the sound of gunfire and witnessed an incredible scene with his wife under the table and Whitty standing over her with a gun in his hand. Forsey threw himself upon the man and the two men struggled.

Forsey himself explained what happened next:

> *Whitty pointed the revolver and was coming for me when I clashed with him. He struggled to get one hand loose but I kept him close to me and prevented him doing so. We wrestled, it must have been for more than five minutes and Whitty seemed determined to try and finish me off.*
>
> *At last however I succeeded in throwing him on his back and held him tightly down for about twenty minutes when a neighbour came and helped me. The mouth of the revolver was at one time touching my ear and a click on the trigger would have ended my life. As it was however I escaped with a bruise on the head and a cut near my ear.*
>
> *I knew from the beginning to the end that it was a fight for life or death and to prevent him firing the revolver I buried my thumb deep into his wrist, even when on the floor Whitty struggled fiercely and when assistance came he was overpowered.*

By the time that Forsey, heroically had managed to overpower Whitty, several neighbours, having heard the shots and commotion, were at the scene and had helped to detain Whitty until the police arrived.

Forsey was especially helped by John Gladwell who lived next door. He heard the shots and, going into the street saw Jeanny Forsey, Eliza's daughter, who told him that a man had shot her mother. They heard another shot being fired and rushed into the house where they saw the two men struggling but Gladwell was able to help Forsey in disarming Whitty.

Sergeant Tighe and other officers arrived at the house and were making enquiries prior to taking Whitty into custody when he asked for a bucket to be sick in. One was supplied to him but he had another purpose for it. He took a handkerchief out of his pocket in which was concealed a razor and before anyone had realised what he was doing, Whitty had slashed his throat causing a large wound in which blood was flowing out. The windpipe was cut through although the jugular vein just escaped. The police at the scene rushed to his aid and tried, as best they could, to bandage the wound but medical assistance was urgently called for and the doctor, as soon as he arrived, ordered Whitty to the infirmary.

Eliza was also taken to the infirmary where her injuries were treated. She appeared to escape relatively lightly having been shot at close range. She had lost blood as a result of the shots and had cuts and bruising but was otherwise fit and healthy and was soon able to be discharged.

Detective Superintendent George Chapman, who had accompanied Whitty to the infirmary searched his clothing and found a loaded cartridge in the right hand pocket of his jacket and three empty cartridges along with a razor case. He formally charged Whitty with the wilful murder of his daughter and the attempted murder of Eliza Forsey to which he replied, 'I have shot Hetty; I told you I would do for the lot of you.'

Rosetta Forsey was laid to rest at Hedon Road Cemetery

Hedon Road Cemetery, where Rosetta Forsey is buried. The author

and on the day of the funeral a large crowd gathered in and around George's Terrace. Several police officers including Inspector Rippon were on duty and about fifty mourners including her husband followed the coffin. The inscription on her coffin read:

Rosetta Forsey died March 28 1901, aged 25 years.

Colonel Thorney, the Hull City coroner opened the inquest into the death of Rosetta Forsey at the St Matthias Mission Room on the evening of Friday, 29 March, the same day that the terrible incidents occurred. However, with Whitty still in the infirmary with the self-inflicted wounds to his throat, the inquest was promptly adjourned and it was hoped that he would soon recover enough to be able to attend.

The coroner was forced into adjourning the inquest several more times, as Whitty was still recovering from the deep wound to his throat. Eventually Colonel Thorney lost patience and decided to bring in legal representation and go ahead with the inquiry with a Mr Gardham representing Whitty.

Harry Forsey told the inquest that he had got to know Rosetta about fifteen months before. Upon being questioned by Mr Gardham, he said that he did not ask Whitty for his consent in marrying his daughter, though he had heard that Rosetta was his favourite daughter.

He said that Whitty had not objected to him dating his daughter, but had warned Rosetta several times that she should

Hull Infirmary. The author

never leave home. He said he believed that Rosetta was Whitty's favourite daughter as she looked after his invalid wife, acting as a nurse. He said that about two months before the wedding, Moses Whitty had told him that he would not allow the marriage to go ahead and that he would sooner 'do for them' and himself. Forsey added that when Rosetta had left home just before the marriage, Whitty became very depressed.

Elizabeth Bushby, remembering the day in question, said that she had heard a terrific scream and went to the back door and shouted, 'Who's that?' No one replied but she heard a further scream followed by silence. Though she heard no shots being fired, she thought she could smell gunpowder smoke and decided to go round to investigate. On getting to the scullery door she saw Rosetta lying in the yard with a broken saucer next to her. Her feet were on the doorstep and she was lying in a pool of blood.

Jane Harrison told the inquest that she did hear the shots being fired and saw Whitty leave the house immediately afterwards. He passed quite close to her and appeared to be very pale if outwardly calm. That same evening, Harrison was being treated at the infirmary for shock and she once again saw the man who had fled from the scene earlier. He was, of course, already under arrest at this time, and was in hospital having treatment for the self-inflicted wound which almost cost him his life.

Eliza Forsey had recovered from her injuries well enough to give evidence to the inquest and she said that about five weeks before her son married Rosetta, Whitty had gone to her house

Below: *St Mark Street as it stands today.* The author

Left: *Frank Forsey, giving evidence at the inquest.* Hull Times

after a quarrel at home and had said to Eliza, 'I neither want her (Rosetta) to court or to marry; I want her for a wife for myself and before she shall marry I will lose my own life.'

Whitty eventually recovered sufficiently to be discharged from the infirmary having been there for eleven weeks and was charged at the police court on 11 June where he was committed for trial at the York Assizes.

At the Assizes the following month, Witty was indicted for the murder and in response to the charge, gave an almost inaudible 'not guilty' plea. Jes Whitty, son of Moses and Rosetta's brother was called for the defence at the trial. He broke down in tears whilst giving evidence and his father joined him.

Mr Marshall, acting for the Crown, said that Whitty was a sane man who was responsible for his actions and that he had intended to take his daughter's life and that of Eliza Forsey.

However, Mr Cautley, addressing the court in defence of Whitty, said that it was one of the saddest cases in which he had ever been called upon to try. He said that the jury may well come to the conclusion that Whitty did shoot and kill his daughter, but a man is not guilty of a crime unless at the time he committed it, he was responsible for his actions and he knew the difference between right and wrong.

He detailed the history of the prisoner and asked the jury to believe that Whitty's daughter was the person that he loved best in the world and that under the circumstances he did not think that the jury could come to the conclusion that he was responsible for his actions at the time.

He added that Whitty had never threatened his daughter before and that the evidence all pointed to him being an affectionate and caring father to his children. He asked the jury to make a charitable view of the case and admit that the prisoner was in a state of frenzy and was therefore irresponsible when he killed his daughter.

The Lord Chief Justice summed up the case and commented upon the painful character of it. He directed the jury on matters of law in regard to the killer's state of mind at the time of the incident and said that from time to time horrific murders were committed by people who were not acting responsibly.

The person committing the murder may be able to recognise the nature and quality of the act, but they may not understand that it was a wrong act.

After retiring for just fifteen minutes the jury returned to deliver a verdict of neither guilty nor not guilty. They found that Whitty had certainly committed the act but that he was not responsible for his actions owing to sorrow and anxiety, so that, in effect, he did not know what he was doing.

His lordship ordered the prisoner to be detained at his majesty's pleasure.

TRIPLE TRAGEDY

IN

EAST HULL.

YOUNG WIFE MURDERED

MOTHER-IN-LAW ALSO SHOT.

ATTEMPTED SUICIDE OF THE FATHER.

Newspaper headline reporting on Moses Whitty's murderous actions. Hull Times

CHAPTER 9

Mystery of Emma Starkie 1901

...he could just make out, in the darkness, the body of a young woman.

Emma Starkie, an attractive twenty-year-old woman lived with her mother at 102 Clarendon Street on Spring Bank and worked as a dressmaker. She was a likeable woman and was a regular attender at the Primitive Methodist Chapel, also on Spring Bank.

Emma Starkie left her home at eight o'clock on the night of Tuesday, 19 January 1901 to take a dress, which she had just completed, to a house in West Parade. She then spent an hour at her auntie's house nearby. Mary Throssell, Emma's aunt said that Emma was in good health and spirits and left her house at

The Victoria Hospital for Sick Children on Clarendon Street exists from the time that Emma Starkie lived on the street. The author

Anlaby Road as it was. Author's collection

about ten past ten with the intention of going to the home of a friend, Mr Mills, a butcher in Portland Street on her way home.

About ten-thirty on the Tuesday night a man called Jonathan Brumby was passing along Caughey Street in the immediate vicinity of Park Street, between Anlaby Road and Spring Bank, only a short distance away from where Emma lived. As he approached a bend in the road he could just make out, in the darkness, the body of a young woman.

Brumby thought initially that the woman had fallen into a fit, but soon noticed, to his horror, that she was bleeding profusely. He called out for help and a policeman, who happened to be passing, soon came to his aid. By the light of the officer's lantern, they saw that an iron instrument had been embedded into the woman's skull, just above the right ear. She was already dead by the time medical assistance arrived.

Brumby did not get a good look at the girl and on returning home he found that his daughter was not in the house. Panicking, he rushed back to the scene of the crime, where police were still dealing with the body, and was relieved to find that it was not his daughter.

Emma was not killed for her money as her pockets were not disturbed. The officer felt in Emma's dress pocket for some identification and found a note there for a Mrs Tiplady, asking her to go and work there. The constable went to Mrs Tiplady's house and was able to identify the dead woman as Emma Starkie. Her body was removed to the police station in Parliament Street and placed in the mortuary to await an inquest from the city coroner.

News of the murder spread throughout the city on the Wednesday morning and crowds of people assembled in Parliament Street, near to where the station was located. Due to the amount of people it was considered necessary to place some constables at the entrance to the station to keep the road clear.

Also, the scene of the murder, about a mile away from Parliament Street, was visited during the day by hundreds of people, some who stood for hours gazing at the bloodstains on the concrete which were still clearly visible. By the afternoon, these marks had become obliterated by the constant tread of the crowd. A mark on a wall, close to where the body was found was also pointed out by many in the crowd. It was seen as an indication that there must have been a struggle there as it was believed that the murderer aimed a blow at his victim and missed her, cutting a piece out of the brick.

Almost every moment somebody struck a match to take a

Parliament Street today. The author

look at the broken brick in the wall. There was also a passage near to where the body was found and it was thought that the murderer may well have lain there in wait for Emma Starkie to pass before making his move.

That afternoon, Mr Wilkinson, the police surgeon conducted a post-mortem of the body. On the right side of the head behind the temple, the head of a hammer hatchet was completely buried in the skull, so firmly that it required some force in order to remove it. The handle had either broken off or been removed.

It was identified as an implement used by people making rafts in the docks, one end used for driving in staples to secure the lashings and the other for cutting the ropes when needed. Similar tools were also used in fixing up lathwork. Police hoped that by identifying so closely the instrument that was used in the murder, it would lead to vital clues in the hunt for the person responsible.

There may have been hundreds of such implements in the Hull area but not many of them would have had a piece missing from its hammer end. It also appeared as if the murder had been premeditated as the hatchet portion of the implement had been recently sharpened to the point that it was extremely deadly.

Police investigations centred at first on Emma Starkie's personal life and they discovered that she was being courted by two men in particular at the time of her death. One of these

Spring Bank in the late nineteenth century. Author's collection

men had his advances rejected by her, leading to a heated argument, and reinforcing the belief amongst many in the police force that jealousy may have been a motive in the murder. However, Emma's mother denied that her daughter was going out regularly with any man.

The inquest into her death was held at the police station in Paragon Street before the coroner JJ Thorney. Jonathan Brumby, of Spring Bank, who found the body, gave evidence, saying that he was just about to pass the bend on the street when he saw something which looked to him like a woman's dress. He said that he took a step away from the body, however, he turned round again, stuck out his foot and felt something soft against it like a woman's dress.

He stooped down and to his horror was face to face with the body of Emma Starkie. He put out his hand and lifted the woman's arm which fell. The woman was lying partly on her face with her back to the wall.

Brumby added that before he found the body he spotted two men and went to the left of the pavement in order to let them pass on his right hand side. He paid no attention to them at the time and thought they were working men due to their clothes.

The inquest continued the following day, this time at the County Court room at the Town Hall and heard from George Bell, foreman of Messrs Earle's iron shipbuilders. He knew the hammer produced very well, saying that it was called a 'hot set' when first made. The tool had come from the Earle's factory

Waterhouse Lane today. The author

and had been missing for a couple of days prior to the murder though nobody had been missing from the works.

Giving evidence, Henry McDonald, said that he had worked at Earle's blacksmiths shop in Waterhouse Lane for about six months. A man called Westerdale had formerly worked at the hearth and the tool had gone missing a few days before the murder. He inquired whether anyone had seen it but did not ask everyone, just those who were in the habit of using it.

William Pickering said that he was also employed at Earle's shop and that he had used the tool himself on 10 January and had often borrowed the tool off Westerdale. Another witness, William Frederick Smith, said that he had cause to go down Caughey Street on the night of the murder and near to the bend where the body had been found, he had seen a man and a woman standing near the wall. The couple were facing each other and the woman had dark clothes and a dark hat. They were talking to each other, with the man saying something to the woman with her replying, 'It's a lie' or 'You're a liar.' Smith went to the police as soon as he had heard about the murder.

The surgeon, Mr Ridsdale, told the inquest that when Emma Starkie was found, she had not been dead for more than ten minutes and said that she had been struck with great violence.

As the inquest proved, the police did at least have several reported sightings to follow up. In addition to the men apparently seen by Brumby and William Smith, on the Wednesday evening, a man went to the station house in Parliament Street and reported to Inspector Wood, who was on duty, that he had seen a man leaving Caughey Street and going into Colonial Street at about half past ten on the Tuesday night and acting in a suspicious manner. The man was dressed in light clothes and had the appearance of a labourer.

He went along Colonial Street and passed into Grey Street, then into Hall Street. He then went into a yard belonging to Mr Branton, a cab proprietor, and was later seen along Spring Bank before crossing into Beverley Road.

In addition, one resident of Caughey Street told the police that he made a nightly practice of examining the dark area of the street with a lantern before retiring to bed. He claimed that when he flashed his lantern at the area on the Tuesday night in question, he saw a man standing there and said that he got such a good sight of him that he would be able to identify the man, even in a crowd.

These reported sightings were faithfully reported by the local newspapers and many rumours swept the city on who was the man responsible. On the following Saturday evening a well-dressed man was arrested by detectives for selling goods in Caughey Street without a peddlers licence. A small mob who witnessed the arrest soon spread rumours that the man had been arrested on suspicion of the murder and a large crowd followed the police officer and the man on their way to the station. However, it was another false alarm and early police optimism gave way to the realisation that the case may prove harder to solve than first appeared, especially as it became more likely that it was a random killing.

The police remained confident that the murder weapon in particular would lead them directly to the murderer, but it was proving a difficult line of enquiry.

The weapon was closely inspected by an engineering firm in the city who said that it was technically known as a warmset, in other words a tool which is commonly used for cutting hot iron. All such tools were thought to be marked, not only by the firm to which they belonged, but also by a workman's private marks to show to which 'fire' in the shop, they belonged. Thus the tool belonging to one fire would be imprinted with a star, another with a cross, another with a flower and so on.

The murder weapon was imprinted with a shell and police were still confident that this mark would narrow down further, those who could be responsible for the crime.

During the investigation the police visited Earle's engine works where they found one of the fire tools which bore the private mark of that upon the hotset used by the murderer. The implement was identified as having been made on those premises but some months previously it had been broken and after that it was not used as a hotset but used for splitting wood. For this purpose a short handle, about ten inches in length was fitted to it.

About three hundred of the workmen at Earle's had access to the implement. However, apart from these men, mates and engineers of the steamers used to frequent the same yard and many others used to go to the yard to have a meal at lunchtimes. All of these people were also permitted to enter the works. Though they would not have had direct access to the implement, the fact that so many people entered Earle's works meant that it was incredibly difficult to narrow down this line of enquiry.

Later in the month there was once again, misguided optimism that the case had been solved when a man was taken into custody after he 'confessed' to the crime. The man, Daniel Chapman, a labourer living in Hodgson Street, was detained on being drunk and disorderly. He told the police that he wanted to give himself up for the murder of Emma Starkie, but they didn't believe him and tried to persuade him to take himself home. He insisted that he was responsible and threatened to kill the officer he was talking to.

Finally, he was taken into custody, but when he woke up the next morning in his police cell, he could not recollect anything of the previous night's events and was soon discharged. The *Hull News* said, 'We understand that when taken into custody he requested the policeman to use him tenderly, as he said he should have to suffer plenty afterwards.'

Another false trail came to an end when a man appeared at the Hull police court charged with impersonating a detective. A man called Thomas Ogden went to the police station on Wednesday, saying that he was a detective who had come down from London at the insistence of a man from near Hull to help in the investigation into the murder of Emma Starkie.

He was initially believed by the police and was taken to the place where the murder was committed and the houses of some of the dead woman's friends. However, his conduct was seen as peculiar by some of the officers working with him and after they questioned him, he was locked up as an impostor.

Emma's mother, and other members of the family were of the strong opinion that Emma was the victim of mistaken identity and as the investigation proceeded the police were also leaning towards this view. It was to become a popular theory amongst officers who were at a loss to explain their failure to arrest the suspect. Having eliminated those close to Emma, somebody with little or no motive would be harder to find and apprehend.

Although a reward of £50 had been offered for any information leading to the arrest of the suspect, police were still no nearer catching the killer. A movement was also set up for a penny subscription in the city which would raise money for a suitable monument over the grave of the murdered girl.

Among the many topics of discussion for those who had gathered in the hours and days after the murder was the exposed nature of Caughey Street. The street was fully built up with houses mainly belonging to the middle classes, yet it was very badly lit with only one lamp covering the whole street. If the street had been straight, one light may have been sufficient, yet there was a bend in the street which led to one corner being in almost total darkness. Unsurprisingly, it was in this dimly lit area that the attack on Emma Starkie took place.

So dark was the south side of the street that Jonathan Brumby, when he approached the place where the murder occurred, almost passed the body without noticing it. He was unable to say, on first glimpse, whether the heap was a bag of rubbish or something else. It was only when he looked closely that he noticed the body.

Caughey Street as it stands today with the bend still visible. The author

The *Hull News* said:

> *It is natural that under the circumstances of delay the town should begin to feel restless. The public are deeply interested in the detection of the criminal meanwhile, let the town authorities look at once at better lighting for the town. We must have more gas lamps in such streets. The bend in the road cast a dark shadow and it was almost impossible to imagine a more dimly lit roadway.*

At the adjourned inquest, the coroner said that the jury could adopt one of two courses. They could express satisfaction at what they had heard and deliver a verdict of wilful murder by an unknown person or they could adjourn the case in the hope that more evidence would be uncovered by the police to enable an arrest to take place. He noted that an application had been lodged with the Secretary of State to offer a further reward. Mr Rivett, one of the jury sounded a note of controversy when he said that he was very struck by the absence of knowledge of Emma Starkie's associates and also her movements as stated by her family.

He said he felt that there was not the slightest chance of the jury coming to know who the murderer was. The coroner said he agreed with much of what Mr Rivett had said and he also felt that the only option open to the jury was to deliver a verdict of wilful murder by person or persons unknown.

It was a case which had many leads. The belief that Emma was dating two men, all evidence of the weapon leading to the Earle's yard and several people helping the police with their enquiries. However, despite the best efforts of the police, the killer of Emma Starkie was never found.

CHAPTER 10

Tragedy of Ada Middleton 1901

The girl had been stabbed in the neck and there was a suggestion of sexual assault.

Hull saw several murders within one year. For example, 1901 saw Rosetta Forsey, Norah Amos and Emma Starkie all lose their life, causing outrage and great shock in the city. Many newspaper column inches were spent ruminating on law and order and why Hull was suddenly producing people capable of the most horrific crimes.

Six-year-old Ada Middleton's young life had not been without difficulty. Her mother and one of her brothers had been sent to the Hull sanatorium so the rest of the family, led by her father Robert, a labourer, of 2 Woodhouse Avenue, Woodhouse Street tried to manage as best they could.

Ada went out to play on Thursday evening, 16 May with her younger brother Harry. Her father had warned them not to leave the street but he had known the pair go onto Reservation Field nearby in order to play, so was not too concerned that he could not see them from inside the house. At about eight o'clock, an hour and a half after they first went out to play,

Crowle Street. The author

Harry returned home alone.

Harry said that Ada had gone off with a man. He said that the man, who had a beard and was of medium height, approached Ada and asked her to help him gather up some flowers on a field belonging to the Hull Corporation on Hedon Road, known in the area as Sandy Bank. Harry began to cry, apparently upset by the man's presence but Ada went with him and had not been seen since.

Robert went out in search of his young daughter looking all over the Reservation Field and the adjacent foreshore until about half-past nine when he called in at the nearby Crowle Street police station to report his daughter missing.

Mrs Hall, a woman who had been helping Robert Middleton look after his children, became alarmed when she heard that Ada was missing and she helped organise a search party.

Other members of the public joined in but any hopes of finding Ada were cut short when her body was discovered later that night. At about ten o'clock, Michael Tevenen, who lived in the neighbourhood, found the body in a nearby yard belonging to the Hull and Barnsley Railway Company adjoining the Western Reservation.

Tevenen had been looking around the Hedon Road and Earle's Street area and on finding the body he struck a match and felt her hand which was cold. He noticed that there was blood on her neck and on her clothing.

The girl had been stabbed in the neck and there was a suggestion of a sexual assault. Superintendent Wardell from Crowle Street station was the first police officer on the scene

Earle's Street, where the Earle's Yard was situated. The author

Castle Street, where the mortuary was situated. The author

along with PC Josia Dawson and they sent for an ambulance although they were already sure that the girl was beyond help.

Dr McWillie attended and confirmed that Ada was already dead. His early opinion was that the right carotid artery had been severed and that death was due to a haemorrhage caused by a wound to the neck. He then arranged for the body of the young girl to be taken away to the Castle Street Mortuary.

A search of the immediate area showed up traces of blood leading to a secluded spot near to where the body had been found and it was thought that the murderer had killed the girl before carrying the body a short way to the place where it was found in an attempt to try and conceal it.

The news spread quickly around the East Hull community and there was great sorrow, especially considering she was such a young girl who had already encountered difficulties in her life. Mrs Hall was especially distraught, having become close to Ada in the few weeks prior to her murder. She said:

> *Oh! She was a bonny creature, she attended the Crowle Street School and was well liked in the neighbourhood. Of rather stout build she was fair with dark eyes and long light hair. She had three brothers.*

People read all about the murder in the *Hull Daily Mail* and the other local newspapers, including the *Hull Times* and the *Hull Packet*, which pointed out where the murder was committed. Inevitably the murder scene attracted crowds all the following day, notably the entrance to the yard. There was interest also in how the murderer managed, in the first instance, to get away with it. It was felt, by locals as well as the police, that after enticing the girl away from her brother and friends, the murderer must have taken her down Woodhouse Street and eventually crossed the Boston Reservation to the place where she was eventually found. Though it was dark, they assumed that somebody must have seen this happen.

Then, in order to enter the deal yard of the Hull & Barnsley Railway Company, the man must have had to go through large gates and it would have been necessary for him to walk, presumably with the girl, through big stacks of timber for

TERRIBLE TRAGEDY IN HULL.

LITTLE GIRL BRUTALLY MURDERED.

Below: *Woodhouse Street today, open and industrial, very different to how it looked in 1901.* The author

Right: *Newspaper headlines the day after the murder.* Hull Times

about twenty yards before reaching one of the most secluded parts of the yard which contained thousands of standards of timber. Her body was found about 200 yards from Hedon Road and perhaps a similar distance from the water's edge.

Blood was found in several parts of the yard, not only in the immediate area where she was found, but also in another sheltered spot about ten yards away from where the body was located. There were no signs of any struggle having taken place.

The inquest into the death of Ada Middleton, held at the Town Hall, heard Dr McWillie, who examined the body at the scene of the murder, confirm that, contrary to early police fears, the little girl had not been sexually assaulted. The coroner said that having examined the wound, he believed that it was caused by an ordinary pocket-knife rather than a sheath knife.

The doctor reported on how he was sent to further examine the body the following morning. He said that the body was cold by this time and added:

> *I only made a rough examination but the wounds were small. The child's face was much smeared with blood. In my opinion after the child's throat had been cut she had been carried a distance of about thirteen yards because traces of blood were clearly discernible on the ground. I am convinced that the injuries were inflicted by a sharp knife. My examination was only a quick one but I cannot state anything further.*

The inquest also heard from Michael Tevenen, who found the body and was one of the people involved in looking for the girl in a search party. He first noticed something light in amongst all the dark wood in the yard, and when attempting to get a better look by striking a match, he immediately saw that he was looking at the body of the missing girl.

He said that she was lying on her left side with her left hand held up and her right hand clenched. Seeing that she was already dead, he was so shocked at the discovery that he stood in the same spot for two or three minutes before calling for the police who he found in Hedon Road. He went back to the spot where he found the girl and remained there until they arrived.

The inquest was then adjourned with the great hope that when it next reconvened, the police would have caught Ada's killer.

Police at the Crowle Street division under Superintendent Wardell took charge of the matter and made an exhaustive search in their attempt to find the murderer. However, the police were hampered by the lack of a motive as random killings are by their nature, far more difficult for the police to solve. Also, their best and apparently only witness, Ada's four-year-old brother, was unable to adequately describe the man who took his sister away.

A couple of days after the murder the police made a significant discovery which, they hoped, would prove crucial in identifying the killer. Found at the murder scene had been a letter, which had traces of blood on it and appeared to have been written in Swedish.

The letter was translated into English and appeared to be from a relation of the recipient and related to purely domestic matters. There was no address on the letter nor a name of the recipient or the sender.

Police, partly because of the letter and also because of the proximity of the murder scene to the Alexandra Dock, believed that the killer may well have been Scandinavian, and they spent much of their time visiting boarding houses and the homes of people who used to take in lodgers. They were also seen more frequently in the 'seedier' public houses in the centre of Hull and at the docks.

Police were quietly confident that the letter would lead them directly to the attacker and continued to watch the shipping patterns at the Alexandra Dock, but as the days passed with the

Alexandra Dock today. The author

murderer still at large, doubts began to emerge about whether or not the letter had been dropped by the killer. There were many within the force who believed that it may have already been on the ground at the scene of the crime and had the blood smeared upon it when the attack took place.

As time went on without anybody in the frame for the murder, there was increasing anxiety amongst the East Hull population, both that the murderer could strike again, but also that the perpetrator of such a hideous crime should be caught and punished.

The *Hull News* reported:

> *Indignation is high amongst the people of East Hull at the ghastly crime perpetrated by some heartless brute. Groups of labourers were to be seen this morning gathered all about the docks discussing the crime, and their feelings can only find vent in wild threats of what they would do should the murderer be arrested.*

The murder of Middleton was compared in the local press to that of Elizabeth Oliver in 1888 who also lived in Woodhouse Street. Oliver's body was found on the Hull & Barnsley railway embankment near to Craven Street Bridge and her killer remained at large.

Middleton's funeral took place on the following Monday and the part of Hedon Road stretching from the Alexandra Dock gate to the cemetery was packed with a massive crowd gathered to pay their respects to the little girl, who was known to many in the tight-knit neighbourhood. The cortège left Woodhouse Street at half past two and when it reached the cemetery there were over a thousand

An artist's impression of the murder scene appeared in a newspaper. Hull Times

Crowle Street Board School.
Hull College Local Studies Unit

people at the entrance and on the walk down to the cemetery chapel.

Amongst those attending the funeral were a number of children from the Crowle Street Board School where Middleton attended. Ada's mother and one of her brothers were still in the sanatorium and were not permitted to attend, though her father, other brothers and other relatives and friends were all present.

As the police investigation progressed, a girl living on a keel in Hull, gave the police another lifeline when she said that she had been approached by a man near to the area where the murder had taken place. She said that the man asked her to help him look for a little girl who has been lost. She agreed but the man turned and tried to attack her. She wriggled out of his grasp and screamed which led to the man running away. The girl also claimed that she saw the man sharpening a knife. She said that he was in his mid-twenties, of medium height with deep blue eyes, clean shaven and he was wearing dark clothes. She added that she was sure that the man was English.

By the following Monday, 27 May, it appeared that real progress had been made when police arrested a man on suspicion of the murder. The arrest came about as a result of some information passed to the police and the man was held at the Parliament Street police station. The next morning he was placed among a group of similarly dressed working men and some of the girls who had been playing with Ada on the evening she disappeared tried to identify the man they saw that night. The girls failed to identify him but he was kept in custody for others to try. However, the man was never

The Rapallo liner from the Wilson Line. Hull College Local Studies Library

positively identified and, with a lack of firm evidence, the police had to reluctantly release him.

The following day a Wilson liner, the *Consuelo*, arrived in Hull from New York and a rumour swept the city that a man on board had boasted to ship mates of how he was the murderer of the little girl. A large crowd assembled at the Alexandra Dock quay and among their number were detectives Mennell and Hall. When the *Consuelo* came within hailing distance of the quay side, the captain was asked if he required the services of the police, he said no but Detective Hall boarded the ship and identified the man who had made the allegations regarding Ada Middleton.

He was interested to learn that the ship last arrived in Hull on the morning of the day that the girl was killed, but soon established that there was no truth in the rumour, and the man was allowed to carry on with his visit to England.

Another line that the police were proceeding with was based on the fact that several descriptions of the man had him as having a spotted face. This description was issued all over the country and a man answering the description was seen trampling through the area a day or two after the murder.

PC Kirby was in the Preston area of Hull when he saw a man, with a spotty face, acting suspiciously. The constable

Victoria Dock. Author's collection

observed him coming out of a haystack in which he had been sleeping and he was immediately taken into custody. However, it was to be yet another false trail as the man had an alibi and was released.

Eventually, the adjourned inquest had to reconvene and the coroner noted that the police had not been able to charge anybody with the murder at that time, despite having questioned many people about the attack. He added that he could not trust himself to speak with sufficient abhorrence of the vile and horrible manner in which the child came by her death. He thought that the jury would have no difficulty in returning a verdict of wilful murder against some person or persons unknown.

The jury agree that further evidence was unnecessary and returned that verdict. The coroner expressed his complete sympathy with Ada's father and family, an expression endorsed by the jury.

The *Hull News* said:

> *The police have not plucked out the heart of the East Hull mystery. It is a pity because Hull is getting quite renowned for its undiscovered murder cases. By this time the murderer is evidently beyond all hope of being caught except by some lucky accident and the probability is that when the consternation and horror which followed the foul deed has subsided we shall hear no more about it, but it will be numbered among the undiscovered Hull murders of the past.*

The Ada Middleton case began with the police very hopeful of making a swift arrest, but as it proceeded, it became apparent that a motiveless crime is so much more difficult to solve. In this case, as with several others, the police were able to investigate many leads, and did have suspects in mind, but the public were only interested in the man responsible being charged and convicted of the terrible murder. Despite the best efforts of the force, that never happened and Ada Middleton's murder remains unsolved.

CHAPTER 11

Killing in his Sleep?
1902

She saw that more blood was pouring from a wound in Bolton's throat and caught a glimpse of the handle of a knife protruding from his clenched right hand.

William Bolton was a married man, aged forty-four, who, although separated from his wife for several months, still saw her regularly. He worked as second engineer on a Hull steam trawler and for some time had been living with his brother in a terraced house in Eliza Terrace, one of the poorest areas of tenement at the Hessle Road end of Campbell Street. He was known to terrace dwellers as Bill Bolton and was renowned for liking his drink, though he was also regarded as good natured and not particularly noisy.

Jane Allen was a single woman, about ten years younger than Bolton, who lived nearby at number 10 Andrew Marvell Terrace. It was described as a 'miserable' small, three-bedroomed tenement in a terrace on the left hand side of Campbell Street from Anlaby Road, close to Holmes' Tannery.

Campbell Street today. The author

There was an air of squalor about the surroundings, with a tiny bedroom and the whole house extremely untidy.

She was the daughter of respectable parents who had a business as slaughterers in Goodwin Street but she, herself, had fallen on hard times and was seen as an 'unfortunate' woman, struggling to make ends meet.

Bolton and Allen had known each other for about a year and it appeared to many who knew them that he was infatuated with his younger female companion. He began to go round to Allen's house on a regular basis when he was home from sea and his wife became increasingly suspicious. Even though the couple were separated, she evidently harboured hopes that there could be a full reconciliation, something that was furthest from Bolton's mind.

Eventually Bolton's wife followed him to Allen's house and caused a scene which resulted in the police having to be called. Despite this, in the weeks prior to 17 October 1902, Bolton had a spell back on dry land and continued to visit Allen several times a week.

Living with Allen for about three or four months had been a widow by the name of Mary Butterick. Friends as well as house-mates, the two women had a night out on 17 October returning home at about eleven o'clock. At roughly quarter past eleven, Bolton knocked on the door which was slightly ajar. Allen asked him what he wanted, with Bolton saying he had just called to see her.

Allen, fearing another intervention from Bolton's wife, tried to persuade him to go home but he refused and invited himself in. He was still calm and for a time the couple began to talk amicably. The women had brought home a large bottle of stout and the three of them began drinking it. Eventually, Allen once again said that she would like Bolton to leave. He again refused saying that he had walked the streets the night before.

The couple began to argue and he became excitable and threatening, refusing to leave the house and shouting, 'I shall not go, I do not want to hit you.'

In desperation Allen then blurted out that she was intending to marry somebody else. She said that she had met a young man called Charlie Nicholson, an engine driver and they were to be married at Christmas. Bolton refused to believe her and thought she was just trying to get him to leave the house.

He took a pin out of his scarf and threw it onto the fire and Allen suggested that he should do the same with the ring that she had previously bought for him. However, he then took off the silver ring and, instead of throwing it onto the fire, placed it on one of her fingers, saying, 'Well if you are, I hope you will be happy for ever.'

Bolton, Allen and Mary Butterick remained downstairs talking for some time, apparently having resolved their differences. Both Allen and Bolton went upstairs at about half past midnight, leaving Butterick to sleep downstairs on the couch in the kitchen and giving her instructions to wake them sometime between six and seven in the morning.

Butterick woke up at about ten to seven the following morning and heard the sound of Allen and Bolton chatting and laughing in her bedroom. She then went back to sleep, waking

Anlaby Road at the beginning of the twentieth century. Author's collection

up at about half past eight, when she heard Allen shouting, 'Oh dear, don't.' Fearing that something was wrong, she ran upstairs to Allen's bedroom where she saw the couple lying undressed on the bed.

However, she quickly noticed a large amount of blood on the bed, staining their clothing, especially Allen's nightdress which was saturated. She saw that more blood was pouring from a wound in Bolton's throat and caught a glimpse of the handle of a knife protruding from his clenched right hand.

It appeared that Bolton had taken hold of a large clasp knife, which he used for cutting up tobacco and which had been left lying in a box by his bedside and stabbed the woman before trying to kill himself.

Butterick picked Allen up to see if she was still alive and she was still breathing when Butterick and Bolton placed her on the floor although she was unable to speak. Butterick got a glass of water and lifted Allen's head to wet her lips and try to revive her. Desperate to try and save her friend's life, Butterick ran out into the terrace, crying 'murder' but nobody came to her aid until she went onto Anlaby Road and saw PC's Burton and Shaw on patrol. They calmed her down and rushed back to the house with her.

When the two policemen arrived at the house they met Bolton coming down the stairs of the property. He made no attempt to escape and they sat him down to determine what had happened. PC Burton was in for a surprise as he had known Bolton for about eighteen years and regarded him as a respectable man. It was noticed by the officers that he had a severe gash on his throat which was still bleeding heavily and a taxi was waiting to take him, along with the police, to the infirmary.

Whilst one officer remained with him in the kitchen, another went upstairs to the bedroom where Jane Allen was still laid on the floor. When searching the room in which the murder was committed, Constable Burton found a knife under the bed. It was open and had bloodstains on it.

Dr Lamb came to attend to Jane Allen but it was too late, she had already died. Examining the body he confirmed that Allen had been stabbed three times in the heart as he spotted three distinct wounds forming the shape of a triangle. He said that the knife must have been pushed in with great force as the whole of the blade penetrated her body. Twice the knife penetrated the heart and once the lungs.

By this time bystanders, who had heard the commotion, were crowding outside the house and they soon got their first glimpse of the suspected killer when Bolton was escorted out by the police to be taken to the infirmary.

He was patched up at the hospital before being taken to the police station where he was charged with the wilful murder of Jane Allen. He had already confessed to the officers, saying, 'I don't know what made me do it' and after being charged, said, 'The inspector needn't have said what he did to me because all I have got to say is, I am guilty.' Later, whilst in his cell with time to reflect, he spoke to PC Burton and said, 'Oh God, I have done Jenny, Charlie.'

Allen's funeral took place at the Western Cemetery in Hull and large crowds assembled, both at the cemetery itself and in Goodwin Street where the girl's parents lived. There were some men who had come to pay their respects but most were women and children who pressed forward in the hope of catching a glimpse of the funeral party. In Goodwin Street itself many of the curtains and blinds were drawn as a mark of respect and it was estimated that about 2,000 people had congregated at the cemetery.

The following Monday a closed cab drove up to the gateway of the Hull Police Court in Hanover Square with William Bolton inside it. The case was still attracting great publicity in Hull and the driver of the cab had difficulty in avoiding some people in the crowds who had gathered in and around the court building, whilst there was a larger crowd waiting around the corner.

When Bolton stepped slowly out of the cab a large bandage was wrapped around his neck and he was wincing in pain. He was in such poor health generally that he had to be held by police until he reached his seat in the courthouse. The large crowd waited outside of court until the eight-day remand was ordered and Bolton left in a waiting cab to return to Hedon Road Gaol.

Hanover Square as it is today, by the side of the Guildhall. The author

He reappeared at the inquest just to confirm his name and address and, with all the evidence pointing towards him, the jury quickly delivered a verdict of wilful murder. Bolton was therefore committed to stand trial at the next Assizes.

At his trial the prosecution strived to convince the jury that Bolton had committed the murder due to his jealousy at Allen's insistence on seeing other men, especially Charlie Nicholson who, she claimed, she was intending to marry.

Butterick told the trial that when Bolton was home from his time at sea, he would go to see Allen three or four times a week, but she was also visited by other men and did not make any commitment towards Bolton.

She said that on the night of 17 October, she and Jane Allen left home at about twenty-five past ten and went to the *Parade Hotel*. She had two glasses of whisky, Allen had two glasses of brandy and they returned home at eleven o'clock, still quite sober. She then told the court of finding Allen's body the following morning.

Mr Mortimer, representing Bolton, said that he was a man of good character and was an honest, hard working man, adding that Bolton never made any attempt to deny his guilt and admitted the crime. However, whilst admitting that he had stabbed Allen, Bolton's counsel set up an extraordinary defence, claiming that he had killed her whilst only semi-conscious through sleep.

In the witness box Bolton said that he was not conscious of having done anything to Allen until he heard her call out, 'Bill, Bill, are you going mad'? He said that he then saw the blood on the bed and, realising what he had done, he tried to take his own life by cutting his throat.

He said that he did not use his knife downstairs but when he got into the bedroom he took it out of his pocket and, having cut some tobacco, placed it open, on the box before he and Allen settled down for the night. He stressed that the couple were on good terms and he did not think anything of the argument they had the night before. He added that he already knew that Allen had other male visitors and accepted the fact.

Contrary to the evidence of Mary Butterick, he claimed that Allen had managed to get out of bed herself and asked her to fetch a glass of water. He said that when Butterick came back with the water he pleaded with her, saying, 'For God's sake Jenny, go and fetch someone.'

He then said that Allen sat up on the bed and said to him, 'Whatever were you thinking about, however, you know that you were not awake because I could not get any sense out of you whatever.' He then said that she gradually became weaker and eventually died.

However, Bolton's evidence was totally at odds with that given by Dr Lamb who said that no person could have spoken after receiving the sort of wounds that she had or indeed lived.

It appeared that Bolton's evidence did not carry much

William Bolton in the dock during his trial.
Hull Packet

weight with the jury who, after about ten minutes deliberation and without even retiring from their box, delivered a verdict of guilty and William Bolton was sentenced to death by Justice Channell.

During his time incarcerated in Hedon Road he was seen by many of his friends and relatives, including his wife and on one occasion by his son Richard and his only daughter Harriet. He was on the training ship the Southampton and she was studying at the Park Avenue Industrial School. It was on this occasion, seeing his children for the last time, that he broke down, too distraught at the thought of his children seeing him in such a place.

Bolton wrote to his wife on the day before his execution, saying:

> *I am very glad to hear the children are all well and I sincerely hope you will try and be a good mother and bring them up in the right and proper way, so that we may all meet in heaven again.*

Bolton was executed just after Christmas in 1902, his executioner was William Billington, assisted by his brother John. Shortly before nine o'clock on a Tuesday morning the Billington brothers entered the condemned cell and pinioned the prisoner. It was only a short distance from the cell to the scaffold and Bolton was unassisted and stood firmly at the drop while the executioners completed their work.

Bolton's wife, who had stood by him throughout the trial despite their separation, was given further bad news immediately after his death sentence was passed as she was, herself, sentenced to four day's imprisonment due to the default on a fine collected for an offence under the school board bye-laws.

CHAPTER 12

Murder within the Hull Back Streets
1909

...Florence ...staggered out of the house, covered in blood.

John Freeman was a short, thick set man aged forty-five who worked irregularly as a labourer and lodged with his brother Robert, also a labourer and Robert's wife Florence at number 4 Kingston Place, Porter Street.

Kingston Place was one of the many short terraces which were approached from Porter Street at the beginning of the twentieth century. It was on the left-hand side of the road, near to Adelaide Street and consisted of about seven or eight houses in the terrace. Number four was a three-roomed house, but was in a state of disrepair and the kitchen was barely furnished.

The three of them had been living in the house for the past two years, coincidentally Robert Freeman had been born in the yard in a house directly opposite the one they were living in. Neighbours spoke highly of Robert and Florence Freeman but were less complimentary about John, who had often been drunk and aggressive to some of them.

In recent times Robert had only casual employment on the

Crossroads between Porter Street and Adelaide Street. The author

Artist's impression of the Queen's Dock in Hull. Author's collection

dockside but neighbours spoke well of him as a husband and a father. The couple had three young children, Florence aged five, Kate aged two and Harry who was just ten months. Florence was only thirty years of age though she looked considerably older, probably through living such a hard life in unhealthy conditions, though drink may have been another factor.

On the Saturday night, 28 August 1909, the three of them, Florence, Robert and John had been drinking together in a nearby pub and were all the worse for drink when they returned home. At about eleven o'clock that night their drunkenness degenerated into an argument between them.

A neighbour overheard Robert say to his wife, 'You've been with him again' and she shouted back 'liar' before all three of them could be heard shouting at each other. Florence kept on repeating the word liar and neighbours heard the noise of scuffling. It appeared that the two brothers were having a fight and there was crashing and banging as if a table had been overturned, before a piercing cry of 'murder' could be heard throughout the neighbourhood.

As blazing rows in the house, and indeed in the yard, happened frequently, neighbours did not take too much notice of the noises coming from the Freeman household and nobody went to investigate until Florence opened the door and staggered out of the house, covered in blood. She somehow found her way back inside and, seeing her struggle, Patrick Gerraghty, a steam trawler engineer, went to help. He went through the front door and, as he ran into the main room, Florence fell into his arms. John Freeman was also in the room, with a bloodstained table-knife in his hand and Robert was trying to disarm him.

Florence had collapsed and lay face down in a pool of blood. She had been stabbed and had a deep wound near to the collarbone and another under her breast. She was deeply unconscious though still alive at this point.

Inside the house the two brothers were still fighting with one another. It had become violent and there was a desperate struggle before John could be restrained and then arrested. Police had already been called to the house and when they arrived they found Robert holding John in the fireplace. Sergeant Boyce seized the man who struggled to get away but he was eventually pushed onto the sofa and held there until he was handcuffed. The police asked John what he had done and he admitted attacking his sister-in-law, adding, 'I hope she is dead.'

Florence was still lying in a pool of her own blood, struggling for life. Her mouth kept opening as if she was trying to speak, but no words came out and Dr Roberts examined her, arranging for her to be taken to hospital immediately though he felt she was already beyond help. He also attended to her husband for a cut on his eyebrow which required two stitches.

As the doctor had suspected, Florence died before reaching the infirmary and with both Robert and John also taken to receive medical treatment, the house was locked and shuttered that night with police staying in the vicinity. They also took possession of some items from the household including the table knife which they believed to be the murder weapon.

John Freeman had been treated at the infirmary for cuts and bruises, but was soon discharged and taken to the central

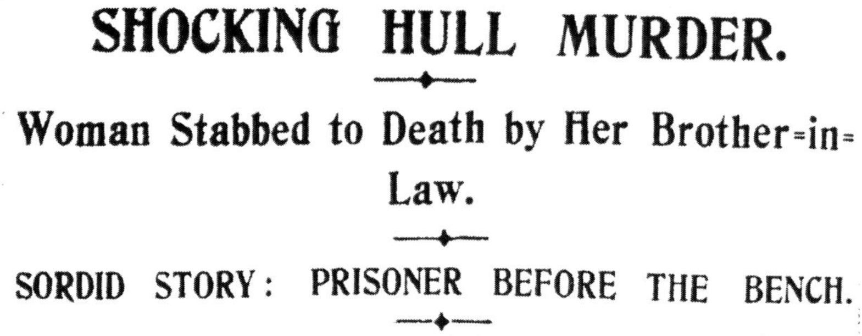

SHOCKING HULL MURDER.

Woman Stabbed to Death by Her Brother-in-Law.

SORDID STORY: PRISONER BEFORE THE BENCH.

Newspaper article reporting on the murder of Florence Freeman. Hull Times

police station. On arrival he once again became violent and had to be restrained by the officers present. He was also drunk and was placed in a secure 'cage' where he was charged with the murder of Florence Freeman. Eventually he calmed down and appeared to appreciate the consequences of his actions.

Robert Freeman, although his injuries did not appear to be severe at the time, did suffer concussion on the brain which left his memories of the Saturday night in question a little hazy. He appeared to have little idea of what happened that night and had to ask the hospital staff why he was being treated at the hospital. News of his wife's death had been kept from him whilst he was in hospital.

Florence and Robert's three children were in the house when Florence was attacked; the baby's cot was in the room where assaults took place whilst the other two children were sitting on the bed upstairs. All three were taken to the homes of neighbours whilst their father was recovering in hospital.

Meanwhile, as the local community began to recover from the shock of having a murder within their tight-knit neighbourhood, details slowly began to emerge over what happened in the house when the three of them returned from the pub. Robert had apparently accused his wife of having an affair with his brother and this was the catalyst for a serious quarrel.

William Gibson said that at about eleven o'clock on the Saturday night, 28 August, he and Patrick Gerraghty were walking down Porter Street when they saw a woman in Kingston Place shouting 'Murder!' They ran into the terrace and heard shouts and screams coming from one of the houses. Gerraghty said that he saw from outside the house the man slash the woman across the neck with something in his hand.

One of the neighbours gave a slightly different version of the events, saying that she saw Florence at about eleven o'clock that night, standing in the yard opposite her house and giving one of her children a drink of water. Then she saw John Freeman returning from the end of the yard and seizing Florence by the hair. A struggle ensued and the woman tried to escape from his grip but he managed to keep hold of her and struck at her with something he held in his hand, which the witness could not identify. Her face became covered in blood and she muttered something before falling to the floor.

The different events left neighbours confused but intrigued and many theories did the rounds with everyone having their own idea as to what happened and why. The consensus amongst them was that drink and jealousy were the two prime motives for the murder with many wondering whether Florence and John really were having a relationship.

Robert Freeman stayed in hospital for treatment for a few more days and his memory slowly began to return. He recalled that on the Saturday morning, he worked at the Queen's Dock and went home for his dinner, finding Florence and John there, so they all ate together. He said that he and his brother then went out for a walk, first to the market, then on to the pier. They popped into the *Rampant Horse* pub for a drink before returning home via Mytongate.

Artist's impression of John Freeman.
Hull Times

Rampant Horse *pub.* Hull College Local Studies Unit

He added:

> *We had our tea together in the house and afterwards we went out again. After a while we went into the Myton Arms. We were friendly in the public house.*

As they were alone the two men got talking and Robert confronted his brother, mentioning that he was becoming uncomfortable about the relationship between John and Florence, saying it wasn't right for a single man.

He went on:

> *My wife was not with us but she had had some drink. I remember going home and I remember having some words with John, but I don't remember anything else after that. Yes, we had some words, I know I said something to him but as to the rest, my mind at present is a blank. I may be able to recall it later but I cannot recollect anything about it now. I wish it had never happened. My brother and I were friendly, he's a quiet little fellow when sober. There is no doubt we had all had some drink.*

Robert added:

> *It was not right of me to keep my brother in the house, but I did it out of kindness. I did not want to see him walking about without anywhere to go or have to go into the workhouse. I am not one to take a lot of drink for a little soon overcomes me. I wish I could remember all but I can't.*

Robert also paid tribute to Florence, saying that she was a good wife and mother and admitted that his brother deserved to be punished for what he had done.

The local newspapers gave blanket coverage to any murder in Hull; they were still comparatively rare and one newspaper reporter went to the scene of the crime in Kingston Place to give an illustration of how some of the city's poorer inhabitants lived. He said that the interior of the house was squalid beyond description and that going into the house where the Freeman's lived, he was met by an offensive odour. There was a table under the window and an old sofa, a few chairs and a broken baby carriage along with one or two prints and ornaments over the fireplace.

Apart from the furniture there was some broken crockery over the floor and a large bloodstain near to the table on which were laid a number of bread loaves. There was only one living room measuring about seven feet square, a bedroom and a small attic, but no inside toilet. In general, the house was in a terrible state with paper peeling off the walls in patches.

Typical back-to-back terrace in Hull. Author's collection

The reporter said:

The whole appearance of the room was one of squalor and neglect. In fact one would not care for a dog to be kennelled in such a place. In fact I am of the opinion that thousands in the city would shudder if they could see the conditions under which these poor people live. It is impossible to overdraw the picture. On entry into the place my senses were coiled with horror at the wretchedness of the surroundings. To any possessed of a spark of sympathy the spectacle is one well nigh heart rending.

The yard contained about fourteen houses and was entered through a tunnel-like passage. When the yard was entered, people found themselves completely built in, standing in a paved passage with houses on each side. With so much of the area being built-up, there was little chance of daylight entering and fresh air was at a premium with disease being rife. The atmosphere was stifling and hot at all times. There was a tap in the middle of the yard which was for the use of all the houses within it and at the far end were the toilets, also for communal use.

The reporter went on:

There are a large number of children playing about and when one realises that a very large proportion of Hull's huge casual labour population exist under these and similar conditions it seems wonderful that the infantile mortality, high as it is, is not much greater. Living amidst such surroundings, it is not surprising that many of the men led an aimless, worthless and drunken life and many of the women led trying lives and are a sad reflection on their sex and to humanity.

On Monday, 30 August 1909, John Freeman was brought to the Hull Police Court before the stipendiary magistrates and charged with the murder of Florence Freeman.

Standing in the dock, without a collar and tie, he appeared a small man with a pronounced forehead due to his receding hairline. His clothes were shabby and he presented a slightly shambolic figure. He looked around all parts of the courtroom without turning his head and had a fixed vacant expression.

The inquest into the death was also held on the Monday, in the inquest room at the infirmary. The prisoner was brought there by cab from the cells at the Central Police Station.

The funeral of Florence took place the following Thursday, 2 September at Hedon Road Cemetery. The coffin bore the inscription,

> Florence Millie Freeman, died August 28th 1909,
> aged 30 years.

Despite their poverty, the residents of Kingston Place managed to collect fifteen shillings to pay for a large floral tribute to Florence and when the funeral procession went through the city centre, a crowd of about three and a half thousand gathered at the cemetery for a brief service.

Her husband, Robert, remained an in-patient at the Hull infirmary, though he was allowed out to attend his wife's funeral. The couple's three children, who had been cared for by neighbours were taken to the 'Ever Open Door' home on

Edwardian postcard showing Beverley Road. Author's collection

Beverley Road, which was part of the Dr Barnardo's institution and it was the intention to eventually transfer them to a home in London.

At his eventual trial at the York Assizes, John Freeman said that he had been suffering from poor health over the past four years and from nervous depression. He had lived with his brother and sister-in-law for two years and said that he had been on good terms with both.

After the jury heard all the evidence they wasted little time in finding Freeman guilty of murder. Mr Justice Bucknall said that drink was at the bottom of it all but that it could not be an excuse for the crime. 'You have taken the life of this poor woman and the law says you must yourself suffer.' Not long after, Freeman, still composed, handcuffed and in the charge of two prison officials, was taken across the courtyard.

Great efforts were made by the Mayor and Mayoress of Hull to gain a reprieve for Freeman and a petition with 6,000 signatures on it was sent to the Home Secretary. However, despite this and the jury's recommendation for mercy, there was no reprieve and Freeman spent his last days in the condemned cell at Hull Prison, waiting with apparent resignation for his fate.

He had said that death was preferable to a life sentence and stressed that he had had no intention of taking his sister-in-law's life. He said, 'It was in a drunken madness that I caused poor Florrie's death.'

John Freeman was duly executed in Hull Prison with Pierrepoint as the executioner; death was instantaneous. As the

PORTER-STREET TRAGEDY.

Jury Return Verdict of "Wilful Murder."

Newspaper headline reporting on the jury's verdict of wilful murder. Hull Times

hour of his execution approached, a large crowd gathered outside of the prison, many of whom were women with shawls covering their heads.

Interestingly, the executioner, Foss William Pierrepoint, a national figure, had spent most of his early life in Hull. He and his brother, John, lived with their parents in Chalk Lane, Hessle Road. Before becoming a hangman he worked on the construction of the Alexandra Dock and he recalled several notorious Hull crimes, especially the *Rising Sun* murder and visited the vessel after the murder out of curiosity.

CHAPTER 13

Three Unsolved Killings
1901, 1873 and 1888

Anne Todd

The death of Anne Todd, aged seventy-eight, in February 1901 did not arouse suspicion immediately. The widow of a farmer, she had suffered ill health as was expected in people of that age at the turn of the last century. However, when police searched their records, they found there was perhaps more to her death than was apparent at the time.

On 20 February 1900, almost a year earlier, Mrs Todd, who lived alone in a house in Hallgate, Cottingham, was found unconscious, having been savagely beaten by someone who was seemingly intent on robbery.

Anne had insisted on not receiving help despite her advanced age, doing all her housework herself. She was in the habit of rising early in the morning so it was a surprise for Herbert Watson Rose, a school attendance officer and vestry

Hallgate, Cottingham at the beginning of the twentieth century. Author's collection

clerk in Cottingham, who lived opposite Mrs Todd, when he saw the curtains drawn and no smoke rising from the chimney on the morning of 20 February. His wife pleaded with him to go and see if Anne was all right and eventually he agreed and crossed the road.

He went round to the back of the house and entered the kitchen. The door leading into the front room was open and there was a lamp burning. On looking behind the back door he saw Anne Todd lying across the floor. There was a large pool of blood there with a set of dentures resting in it. He lifted her head, believing that she was already dead, but to his surprise she let out a low moan. He went out into the street and tried to summon help.

Police were called and they found that the whole house had been ransacked with pots broken and house contents scattered about the floor, though nothing appeared to have been stolen. Officers surmised that people had entered the house with the intent of robbery, but seeing how badly hurt she was, they had panicked and left the house with nothing.

Herbert Rose also contacted Dr Galt, who had been Anne Todd's GP for about thirteen years. He saw that Anne had a swollen face and neck, which were covered, in bruises. Her eyes and the back of her head were also swollen and he also noticed a fracture to the right of the head which may have extended to the left ear.

The injuries had not been caused by a fall and had certainly not been self-inflicted. They were at least twelve hours old and had occurred the previous night. He believed that a heavy instrument had caused the injuries, possibly a poker which had been found in the same room.

Anne Todd was left with severe injuries to her head and she was unconscious for several days. However, she managed to make a slow recovery and after a long recuperation, in hospital and at home with help, was eventually able to get about. She was soon able to take the occasional walk though she often felt dazed and there was general concern for her long-term safety.

As for the night that she was attacked, her memory was imperfect, though she was to remember that one evening a man and woman came round to her house and, after asking them what they wanted, the man replied 'I'm going to do for you.' She said that he must not but could not recall what happened after that.

With her recuperation progressing she continued to live alone in Cottingham and had a former servant come to visit her to check that she was coping.

This was the situation until 23 November 1900 when she moved in with her brother-in-law, Luke, who was a cycle dealer and lived at 362 Anlaby Road in Hull. On 5 December, she was again taken ill and was attended to by Dr Galt but her condition continued to deteriorate and she died on 25 February 1901.

With the knowledge that she had been savagely beaten a year earlier, police decided that an inquest should be held.

On the Tuesday night after her death, Colonel Thorney, the Hull coroner, held an inquest at the *Newington Hotel*. Dr Galt, on being questioned, said that death was due to cerebral failure triggered by malnutrition, the inability to take in food. In other words, he said it was due to natural causes accelerated by the injuries she sustained a year earlier. He added that Anne Todd's brain had never regained its strength after the original attack

Another view of Hallgate from the same period. Author's collection

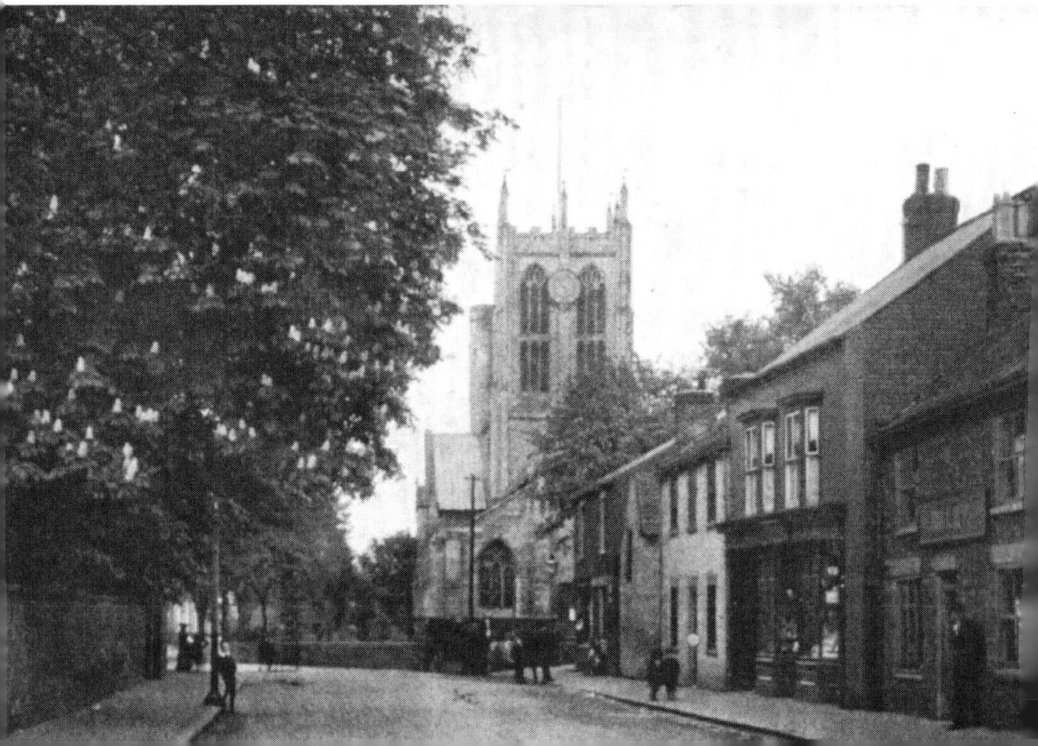

and her statements could not be relied upon or given before a jury.

He added that he had found marked traces of the injuries she sustained when she was attacked the year before. With little other evidence before them, the jury duly returned a verdict of wilful murder by person or persons unknown. Despite the finding, the police never did find the couple who, Anne Todd claimed, had threatened her in the days before the original attack.

Joseph Cowling

William Cowling, a cabinet maker by trade, lived with his wife Elizabeth at Rose Ann's Place in Hill Street. The couple had a two-year-old son called Joseph, who they believed to be independent enough to be left playing with other youngsters in the street. No harm had ever come to him as it was felt to be a safe neighbourhood.

William left home on Monday afternoon, 7 April 1873 at about one-thirty to go to work leaving Elizabeth and Joseph at home on the sofa. Elizabeth gave her son permission to play outside with friends and was unconcerned, as he had done this several times before. The little boy was wearing a red flannel shirt; a scarlet petticoat attached to a light waistcoat and a green frock with dark spots. Over this he had a white pinafore and a grey beaver hat with a feather on one side.

After an hour or two Elizabeth called him in but was a little worried to find that there was no trace of him after searching inside the house and out. Becoming more frantic she knocked on the doors of her neighbours but nobody had seen him.

William Cowling was sent for at the shop he was working in at about half past six to be told that his son was missing. He rushed home and started to search the immediate neighbourhood, even enlisting the help of Hull's town crier to see if the boy could be found and, along with about a dozen other neighbours' searched the locality right through until two o'clock the following morning. That was when he informed the police that his son was missing.

Henry Golding, aged nine, had gone out on the Tuesday

Fountain Road as it stands today. The author

morning at about seven o'clock to catch a lark which had escaped from a cage at his father's house. The bird flew over some trees and came down underneath a hedge in a field in Granger Street near Fountain Road. Henry and his friends, who had come out to help him, stopped and discovered that about two or three yards away from where the bird was found was a small pool of water. To their horror, they saw that lying face-down in the pool, was the body of a small boy.

There were about five inches of water in the pool, which formed part of a ditch, which had been filled up with clay. It appeared to have been deliberately dug and the water came up to the ears of the boy, but did not cover his head. The boys could see that Cowling was dead and they ran across the road towards two bricklayers to tell them what they had seen. The men then phoned the police.

PC Canty rushed to the scene where a large number of people had already gathered to see what had happened. He quickly came to the conclusion that he was dealing with a murder inquiry. The child, despite being fully dressed when leaving the house, was found naked apart from a pair of socks and laced-up boots.

Some pieces of a hedge, apparently broken off, were lying against the body and there were men's footmarks on either side of the hole, though it was impossible to determine whether they were recent or not. Some other twigs had been broken off the hedge and placed on the body in an apparent attempt to hide it.

Mr T Evans, the police surgeon saw the body on the Tuesday morning at about half past eleven. Some pieces of thorn bush and dead leaves were embedded in the hair of the dead boy but there were no marks of violence on the body apart from a scratch on the knee. Mr Evans found that the windpipe and air tubes were full of froth and contained a substance which turned out to be vegetable matter such as frozen stagnant water. Joseph's stomach was also full of water, which contained the same vegetable matter.

There were about seven inches of water in the hole in which he drowned and the hole had high sloping sides meaning that once inside it would have been very difficult for the little boy to escape. There was sufficient water in the hole for the boy to drown so the police tended towards the theory that he had been forcibly pushed into the hole and possibly kept there against his will.

A fortnight later an inquest was opened at the police station in Parliament Street on the death of Joseph Cowling. The police told the inquest, which was presided over by JJ Thorney, that in the two weeks since Cowling's death, no fresh evidence had come to light. A brick pond, near to the place where the body was discovered, had been dragged but nothing had been found.

An old lady who lived nearby on Fountain Road said that she heard the scream of a young child at about one o'clock on the Tuesday morning. She said that the scream came from a distance as if from a child in one of the nearby houses in the terrace.

The coroner said that it would be advisable for the jury to come to a verdict that day so that a reward may be offered. He pointed out that if the child had managed to take some of his

Parliament Street police station. The author

clothes off himself, they would probably been found nearby and also if the child had been walking around without any clothes on, he would have attracted attention. The jury therefore returned a verdict of wilful murder against some person or persons at present unknown.

The *Hull Times* said:

> *It is to be hoped that the cruel perpetrator or perpetrators of so cold-hearted a crime as murdering a child for the paltry value of his clothes will not escape justice.*

Sadly, the *Hull Times* did not get its wish and this was another investigation, which was to prove fruitless for the Hull police force. Despite many hours on the case, the murderer of Joseph Cowling was never found.

Wincomlee today, near to Fountain Road. The author

Elizabeth Oliver

Elizabeth Oliver was the thirteen-year-old daughter of Charles Oliver, an engineer, who lived in Florence Terrace, Woodhouse Street. Charles and his wife had five other children; the eldest child being aged fifteen and the four others all still living at home.

Elizabeth's parents went out at about seven o'clock on the evening of 7 February 1888, leaving her at home with their other children. A short time after, Elizabeth went out to play.

A little after half past seven, Elizabeth Oliver called at the house of a friend called Sewell who lived across the road to see if she wanted to play outside in the street. The father of her friend refused to let his daughter out as it was already late so Elizabeth told her that she intended to go to Craven Street to see another girl. She left the house of her friend and turned the corner of Woodhouse Street. That was the last time she was seen.

Her parents returned home at about ten o'clock and, discovering that Elizabeth was out, began to make enquiries. With nobody having seen her for some time they eventually reported her missing to the police and, together with a police officer, Charles Oliver searched the railway lines and the immediate neighbourhood. Having gone along the North Eastern lines without success they went upon the Hull & Barnsley embankment. Here Oliver said to the officer, 'If we find the poor lass is hurt we shall find her chucked at the back of the fence', a remark which puzzled the officer.

The search continued through much of the night and carried on in earnest as soon as it was light the following morning. However, it ended in tragedy at about ten o'clock that morning when her body was found on the railway line by a labourer named Robert Wallis.

Elizabeth's body was discovered at the foot of the Hull & Barnsley Railway embankment near to Woodhouse Street and it was thought that she had been thrown bodily over the wooden partition separating the road from the embankment and there was also evidence that the girl had been brutally assaulted. It was believed that she was attacked a short distance away from where she was found and that, whilst unconscious, she was carried over to the embankment. Her boots were clean suggesting that she had been carried to the place where she was found.

As a police surgeon soon identified, there were fingermarks on the body pointing to the fact that the windpipe had been grasped by a strong hand, whilst on the face there were a number of bruises and there seemed little doubt that death was due to strangulation.

There was also a large bruise on the dead girl's temple which indicated that she was hit by a heavy blow to the head, either by a fist or as the result of a fall. On each side of the nose were seen the imprints of a person's fingers. It appeared that the murderer had put his hands on her face immediately in order to stop her screaming out and ultimately to stop her breathing.

Another reason why the police assumed this to be a murder investigation was that the scene of the crime was a very isolated spot and it was thought unlikely that the young girl would have left home and gone to such a bleak place without having been forced into doing so. She was described by many who knew her as being very well behaved and cautious and nobody thought it likely that she would willingly accompany a man to such an isolated spot.

There was an air of grief around the Hedon Road area of Hull as well as shock and disbelief that a young innocent life had been taken. There was more shock when the results of the post-mortem became known. Conducted by Dr Pigeon, it confirmed evidence of foul play and the east Hull community knew there was a murderer in their midst.

There were large expectations of an arrest in the case within a few days of the murder taking place but these hopes gradually eroded as the police found solving the case more difficult than was perhaps initially thought.

On the Thursday night police were still at the scene searching the local area but were finding it difficult to find any sign of the man they were looking for. There were no marks on the ground to indicate a struggle.

When employees at the nearby Earle's factory left for home on the Thursday, each man was questioned by Detective

Inspector Clapham and several assistants. Police later revealed that they wanted to speak to a boilermaker in the yard. The man in question was at work as usual on the Monday, Tuesday and Wednesday but it was not known if he turned up for work on the Thursday morning, but he was certainly not in the yard by the Thursday afternoon. Also, since that time he had not been seen, leading to police suspicions that he may have been involved.

The police had further leads to work on. A little girl called Fillingham, who lived in Clarence Street off Hedon Road, had to run an errand to a house close to the Olivers' home the night that Elizabeth disappeared. She delivered the message and was about to run home when she was accosted by a man who was standing against one of the houses in Florence Terrace. The man asked her to go to the bridge with him and said that if she went with him he would give her a penny. He was dressed in a blue jacket, a cap and had working trousers on.

Woodhouse Street today. The author

The dead girl was discovered on Wednesday morning and about noon on the same day a man 'of peculiar appearance' was seen on the opposite side of the street to that on which Florence Terrace was situated. He was said to have been very agitated and after partly crossing the street, twice went back. Eventually he did cross the road and knocked on the Olivers' door to ask if Elizabeth was in and if he could speak to her.

He did eventually speak to her but nobody, including Elizabeth's parents, got a good view of the man or could hear what they were talking about, although one or two neighbours saw him from a distance and were able to give the police a description.

A woman in Arundel Street also came forward and said that she saw the murdered girl on the night in question, standing on the railway crossing at the bottom of Woodhouse Street talking to a man.

Two weeks into the case and the police were still working around the clock to try and make an arrest.

The *Hull Times* stated:

> *The man has yet to come who will succeed in drawing aside the curtain and revealing the murderer to the public gaze and whether it will be in our day and generation remains to be seen.*

The paper also cast a certain amount of doubt on Charles Oliver despite him appearing to have an alibi, having been out with his wife on the night in question. The *Hull Times* said that from the moment his daughter was known to be missing, 'Charles Oliver appeared to be possessed by a sort of presentiment that some serious evil had befallen her.'

The *Hull News* also appeared to cast suspicion on him, commenting that before he knew the fate of his daughter, he had the theory that she was murdered in a house or shed nearby before being thrown over the fence onto the railway embankment:

This is a truly remarkable and even prophetic statement from the part of the father for it would appear that at the time he could have had no knowledge of the outrage that had been perpetrated on the girl.

Mr J Thorney, the Hull Borough coroner, opened an inquiry, held at the *Oriental Tavern*, Hedon Road and Charles Oliver's comments attracted the attention of the jury here too. He could only account for his remarks by saying that it was made on instinct. The jury were also interested in a statement that Oliver made to the police saying that the finding of the murderer would do neither him nor Elizabeth any good. However, he did also say that if he had it in his power to put down £100, he would give it to the person who found the murderer to help bring him to justice.

The jury nevertheless put the father through quite a severe cross-examination, eliciting from him the information that he had arranged to go to a steamer on the Alexandra Dock for the purpose of identifying a man who he suspected of the murder. However, he did not go, explaining that he could not get from Hedon Road in time.

The *Hull News* stated:

This is unfortunate, for this failure to keep a most important appointment may have enabled the murderer to get clear away. From the evidence given, the jury could not have the slightest hesitation in returning a verdict to the effect that the deceased had been murdered.

As the report indicated, with no other firm evidence linking Oliver himself or anyone else to the death of Elizabeth Oliver, the adjourned inquest delivered a verdict of wilful murder against some person unknown. The *Hull News* said there is a saying that murder will out but the paper cast doubts on this as it pointed out that there were several undiscovered murders relating to Hull alone.

In early March, about a month after the murder of Elizabeth Oliver, another attack was reported to the police at the station in Crowle Street. William Cakes was playing on Hedon Road near to Wyke Street at about six-thirty on 5 March along with three other boys. They were all playing tig and the three other boys went into Zicken's coffee house to hide from Cakes. They hid for a little while, but realising that he had not followed them in, they left and went outside to look for him.

They soon found him lying unconscious on an embankment, a piece of vacant land belonging to Hull Corporation, adjoining Hedon Road. The boy was taken home by his friends and his parents sent for a doctor. Upon examining the boy, the doctor found that hc had received a heavy blow to the right temple though it was impossible to say how the wound had been caused.

Cakes remained unconscious until about eleven o'clock at night, but he then awoke and his memory of what happened to him earlier in the night was not affected. When asked how he had come by his injuries, he said that as he was running after his friends, a man stopped him and asked if he was short-sighted. He replied by saying no, but the man said that if the boy would go up the bank and see if there was a vessel on Earle's Slip he would give him a penny.

He did run up the bank but was quickly followed by the man and when he reached the top the man grabbed him and threw him down. The boy tried to get up but was hit by a blow on the right temple.

The boy was able to give the police a description of his attacker. He said that the man was dressed respectably and had a moustache and that he would recognise him again. He added that there were quite a few people on the roads at the time and was sure that somebody would have noticed the man. However, as time progressed nobody was arrested for the attack on the boy and the possibility emerged that the same man who killed Elizabeth Oliver was responsible for the latest outrage.

Despite so many leads, the police failed to find the killer of Elizabeth Oliver or the person responsible for attacking William Cakes. Elizabeth's father was under suspicion for comments made, a man had left the Earle's shipyard mysteriously and there had been other sightings of men in the area acting suspiciously, but nobody was charged with her murder. There were also similarities between this case and that of Ada Middleton who was also killed in the Hedon Road area thirteen years later.

There was a long gap between the two murders, but both were little girls from the same area of East Hull, who had gone missing to be killed, presumably in a motiveless attack. Both investigations also centred on the nearby Earle's factory and the Alexandra Dock. Of more significance is the fact that both murders remain unsolved to this day.

CHAPTER 14

Nine Suicides
1881-1924

Due to the great disapproval surrounding it, suicide was a relatively uncommon event during the Middle Ages. However, suicides and suicide attempts did occur, prompting the authorities of the time to consider a suitable reaction to it. It was eventually agreed that self-harm was a sin and should be prevented if at all possible.

The term 'suicide' was first coined by Walter Charlton in 1651 as a bid to rid it of the criminal and sinful associations which had previously stuck to it. The term did become common use even if Charlton's bid at moral sanitisation failed. Many thinkers in the eighteenth century attempted to justify suicide, some saying for instance that such acts were not a sin since everyone had the right to do what they wished with their own life.

However, the progressive thinkers of the eighteenth and nineteenth century were in a minority as passing of the years saw a hardening of the position towards suicide. Aristotle had argued that those who attempted suicide should be punished and it was no surprise to find that laws were introduced in the early nineteenth century to punish those who attempted suicide or who assisted others to end their lives.

While the upper classes were usually excused punishment, the lower classes could expect a sentence of ten days, with compulsory counselling from a clergyman. Subsequently even stiffer sentences were imposed.

The sociologist Emile Durkheim blamed the 'anomie' of modern industrial society for an increase in suicides but the process of industrialisation cannot be entirely held to blame since suicide rates were highest in the old county towns. At this time suicide continued to be associated in the public eye with sin but the finding that it also showed a strong association with alcohol abuse, poor physical health and poverty sensitised the public towards a more sympathetic and understanding attitude.

Hull had its own problems with alcohol, poverty and poor public health and it is no surprise that suicides were prevalent in Hull in the late nineteenth, early twentieth centuries.

James Henry Walker

Glancing through a window as he came downstairs on a Monday morning in September 1902, Harry James Walker, a butcher, who traded at 278 Hessle Road, was horrified to see his father, James Henry Walker hanging in the shop. Through the window which enabled customers to be seen from the kitchen, Harry was not able to get a perfect view, but running into the shop he found that his father was dead and was hanging from a rope attached to a meathook.

Harry shouted out for assistance and was helped by a passer-by who helped him cut down the body. Dr Tireman was immediately sent for and confirmed to Harry that his father was already dead.

278 Hessle Road as it looks today. The author

The Star & Garter, *still standing today.* The author

James, who was aged fifty-seven, hanged himself from a piece of rope with his feet about two feet from the ground, having climbed up onto a small stepladder. It was estimated that he would have been hanging for about forty-five minutes before being found.

An inquest into the death was held later on the Monday at *The Star & Garter Hotel* where Harry said that he last saw his father at about five-thirty on the Sunday evening when he had appeared depressed. He said that his father had business troubles and had been increasingly anxious during the past few weeks.

Emma Walker, James's widow told the inquest that he got up as usual on the Monday morning at about quarter to six and went downstairs, though he was complaining of pains in his head.

The jury, after careful consideration, found that Walker had hanged himself whilst of unsound mind.

It later emerged that Walker had been an investor in the London & Yorkshire Steam Trawling and Fish Carrying Company which had gone into liquidation and had lost a great deal of money as a result. He clearly had that on his mind in the days and weeks leading up to his suicide.

Richard Simpson

The suicide of Richard Simpson on 24 September 1902 stunned the city, as he was one of the best known men in the Hull fish trade and a former sheriff of the city. Simpson, a widower aged fifty-four, was a smack owner and fish merchant living at 115 Coltman Street in west Hull.

Just before midnight on 23 September, George Simpson, Richard's son saw his father in the dining room before going to bed. He seemed in reasonable health and was quite cheerful, though he had complained of worrying pains in his chest and throat and he also had significant business concerns.

A little after eight o'clock the following morning, the housekeeper, Harriet Davis, woke George up. She then went to Richard's bedroom but noticed that the bed was empty. She

The row of houses in Coltman Street including number 115. The author

called George who searched the house, eventually opening the door to the billiard room where he found his father's body suspended by a rope (such as those used for making fishing nets) from one of the girders. He cut his father down and telephoned a doctor who arrived only to confirm that Richard Simpson was dead.

The inquest opened at the *Criterion Hotel*, Hessle Road, later that day before Colonel Thorney, the City Coroner. Ironically, in the room in which the inquest was held had hung a large portrait of Simpson in his sheriff's robes, testimony to the respect in which he was held by the city of Hull.

The inquest heard that Simpson had become severely stressed due to business concerns in recent months. He had made a great success of the Humber Steam Trawling Company and buoyed by his success, also formed the London & Yorkshire Steam Trawling and Fish Carrying Company.

However, this was to prove his downfall as he had agreed to act as a guarantor for the company which subsequently fell into severe financial trouble. The company was forced into liquidation and Simpson was hit by an Assizes action in Leeds

The Criterion Hotel, *Hessle Road.* The author

in which he was ordered to pay £30,000.

The coroner said that it was certain that he had come by his death by his own hand. He had suffered from heavy pecuniary loss and it was for the jury to decide whether he had hanged himself whilst of unsound mind or otherwise.

The coroner briefly reviewed the evidence and the jury returned a verdict stating that Simpson had indeed committed suicide whilst being of unsound mind.

Five days later, on Saturday, 29 September, Richard Simpson was laid to rest. The curtains in most of the houses on Coltman Street were closed as a mark of respect to his family and soon after one o'clock, a large number of people gathered in the neighbourhood as the coffin was taken out of number 115.

On top of the coffin lay a number of floral tributes as the procession went towards the cemetery church.

Simpson was perhaps the first major public figure in Hull to have killed himself and there was a palpable sense of shock in the city for several days after, whilst the news was digested.

Robert Reginald Rigby

Robert Reginald Rigby, a seventy-two-year-old man living at 35 Newbridge Road, Holderness Road, committed suicide by strangling himself with a leather strap in November 1903. Rigby, who had been a widower for five years, was living at the home of Annie Shay as a lodger while her husband was at sea.

He generally spent his time reading the newspaper and smoking, though he had been out for the day on the Sunday, returning home late and retiring to bed at eleven o'clock. The following morning Shay called him at about ten o'clock in the morning as he was late in coming downstairs.

She went into his room and, to her horror, found him in a sitting position by the side of the bed with a strap round his neck which was fastened to a bedpost. She ran down the stairs and into the street, screaming for someone to help her. A coalman called Chapman, who lived in Studley Street, was nearby and rushed into the house. He quickly released the strap from the neck but the body was stiff and it was apparent

New Bridge Road as it stands today. The author

that Rigby had been dead for some time.

Rigby was usually a cheerful, good-natured man but it was clear to people who knew him that he had been troubled lately as a substantial allowance that he had been entitled to as a cattle trader, had not been received. He was concerned that he would be ruined financially if the issue of allowance was not resolved and was especially worried as he did not want to leave the Shay household, having nowhere else to go. He had also been receiving money from a family friend but for some reason this had also been stopped.

The inquest into his death heard that though an elderly man, he had been in generally good health although he had been treated by a doctor recently for an abscess.

Giving evidence to the inquest, Annie Shay said that Rigby had once threatened to kill himself if he could not remain a lodger in her house, though she maintained to the court that she had never once said anything to make him think that he was in danger of eviction. She spoke of finding him at the side of his bed with his head dangling down and his hands by his knees. He had a strap around his neck but she did not notice that it was fastened to the bedpost.

The jury found that he had committed suicide but there had been no evidence to ascertain the state of his mind at the time.

Holderness Road in the early twentieth century. Author's collection

Cornelius Horton

Cornelius Horton, a police constable with the Hull & Barnsley Railway Company, living at 11 Alexandra Terrace, Londesborough Street, was charged with attempting to commit suicide on 6 April 1901.

During the daytime of 6 April he was in the *Clarenton Hotel* on Londesborough Street with two friends, John Moore and Albert Chadwick.

He left the pub at about one-thirty in the afternoon and the three of them all went to Horton's house nearby. Horton left the other two downstairs and was upstairs for such a long time that his friends became concerned. They searched the house for him and found him in the bedroom.

Horton drew a blade from his pocket and cut his throat inflicting a small wound. Moore said, 'For god's sake what are you doing? Be good for your wife and children's sake.' He managed to grab the razor off him but Horton then grabbed a knife and shouted, 'I mean it!' His two friends managed to grab the knife and call the police with PC Coverdale coming to arrest Horton.

It emerged that Horton had previously tried to take his life

The Clarenton Hotel, *Londesborough Street.* The author

by strangulation and had a habit of depression. He was initially remanded in custody for eight days, but when he was brought back to court, was sent to the asylum to determine whether or not he would be allowed to live independently again.

John Henry Emes

On 16 December 1881 an inquest was held at the *Waterloo Inn* on Wellington Lane into the death of John Henry Emes who committed suicide by shooting himself with a revolver. The inquest was conducted by Mr JJ Thorney, the borough coroner, who swore in the jury and said that their duty would be to determine how the man came by his death.

Aged forty-three, Emes was a ship owner and ship broker who lived at number three Wellington Terrace on Beverley Road. He was also the consul of Uruguay and for years had been chairman of the Market Place Ward Ratepayers Association. On the Tuesday morning, 16 December, he was found lying unconscious in his bathroom with a pistol by his side. Medical assistance was called for but he was dead before he could be treated.

Wellington Lane today. The author

Giving evidence to the inquest, Samuel Aston, a shipping agent, who worked alongside Emes at the firm Hammond, Emes and Co as a clerk and latterly as a partner, said that up until recently Emes had been a very even tempered man but a change had been noticeable in the last few days.

According to Aston, he would bury his face in his hands and had a wild and flushed appearance and he was noticeably restless and walked up and down the office a great deal. He also became very irritable which was also out of character. He had been ill for some time with what Aston thought was a nervous condition, but he also suffered from a bronchial infection.

He was not a big drinker and Aston was not aware of any business trouble which specifically would have caused him to be depressed. Aston last saw Emes on the Monday evening in his office. He knew that Emes had a revolver and that he sometimes carried it around with him to guard himself as he was occasionally forced to carry large amounts of money around with him, sometimes as much as £1,000.

Emma Frokingham also gave evidence to the inquest. She was a cook for John Emes and said that she had also noticed a change in his manner lately. He had become depressed and she was at a loss to explain why his state of mind had changed. On the Tuesday morning she said that Emes had left some of his breakfast uneaten and returned upstairs. One of his children came down and had told Frokingham that her father was making a strange noise upstairs.

She went upstairs to see what had happened and tried to open the bathroom door. As she did, she could see one of his slippers. She moved the foot, opened the door and found him partly on the seat of the toilet and partly on the floor, breathing hard. She noticed the pistol lying on a mat in the closet and screamed out to Emes's wife who called Dr Briggs.

When the doctor arrived, just after nine o'clock, he and Emma Frokingham carried Emes and laid him on a couch but he died after about five minutes. Briggs told the inquest that Emes was bleeding profusely and found that the blood was coming from the right temple. There was also a mark of gunpowder on his temple.

Briggs also said that the skull had been fractured by the gunshot wound. In the glass of the bathroom window there were two holes; one which was clean through the glass and the other which had grazed the woodwork before going through the glass. He said that this proved that Emes had shot himself as the fracture of the window showed that the gun could not have been fired from outside of the house.

Dr Briggs also shed light on a possible motive for the suicide. He said that on the morning of the 16th, Emes had received a message saying that the condition of his favourite daughter, who was living in London and had been ill for some time, had deteriorated. The doctor speculated that this news, allied to general depression may have been the reason for Emes choosing that day to take his own life.

The jury duly recorded a verdict of suicide whilst in an unsound state of mind.

Edward McMahon

Suicides in prison, whilst not unheard of, were comparatively rare, so the case of 'Fanlight Jimmy' attracted great publicity in 1924.

Edward McMahon was dramatically arrested on Thursday, 6 December 1924 in the early hours of the morning and at Hull Police Court was charged with breaking and entering into 37 Chariot Street. An officer noticed that the fanlight of the shop was open and saw a set of footprints. PC Robinson climbed up the fanlight and shouted 'Come out of it!' McMahon came out and said to the officers, 'It's not a bad job when you can get away with it.'

McMahon, aged twenty-five, had lived at 49 Osborne Street and was a notorious character who had been known to the police for some time and had a particular tendency to enter properties by the fanlights, hence the name 'Fanlight Jimmy'. He had previously been in prison for two periods of three months each time.

After being remanded by magistrates, McMahon was removed to Hull Gaol, Hedon Road, where he was placed in a cell. He was not considered to be a particular suicide risk but, as with all prisoners, the prison authorities took precautions and kept looking through the hatch in his cell.

He had spent most of the Friday in his cell and had been taken a meal at about five o'clock in the afternoon. A prison warder entered his cell on the Friday night at seven-forty with his late meal and found him hanging by a piece of cloth torn from a sheet, one end being tied to a bar on the cell window and the other round the man's neck.

The warder lifted McMahon to take the weight off the rope and called for assistance. Two warders came to his aid and McMahon was cut down and taken into the corridor where artificial respiration was tried until the arrival of a doctor who pronounced him dead.

The inquest into his death was conducted at Hedon Road jail by the Deputy Coroner, Dr Eric Jackson.

It heard that after fixing the improvised rope in his cell, McMahon had apparently jumped off a stool and in the opinion of the warder, he was still alive when cut down. The warders said that there was nothing in McMahon's manner to indicate that he wished to take his own life.

His sister said that she last saw him alive the Wednesday before, the day before he was arrested and was quite cheerful in his manner. Again there was no suggestion that he intended to take his own life. However, she thought that his arrest and subsequent imprisonment had undoubtedly led to him taking his own life as she knew that he feared another spell in prison.

In returning a verdict of suicide, the foreman of the jury said that they considered that McMahon was sane at the time he committed the act.

Dr Arthur William Stone

Dr Arthur William Stone, a well known doctor in Hull, lived and practised at 455 Hessle Road. Aged about fifty, he was single and though not born in the city, he had been a resident in Hull for over ten years and was well respected by many inside his profession and other members of the public with

Number 455 Hessle Road was demolished to make way for this supermarket.
The author

whom he had come into contact.

His housekeeper, Anne Hollingsworth went to bed at about ten-twenty on 3 December 1902 and he followed at about eleven-thirty. The following morning she went to his bedroom and tried to wake him by knocking on the door. She found this a little strange as he was usually up before she was.

There was no response so she then went into the room to see him in bed, apparently asleep. She shook him but he still did not wake up, so she sent for his partner Dr Muir, who arrived shortly, only to find that his colleague was dead.

PC Leighton was called by the doctor and discovered, on the table by the bed, a glass and a bottle containing prussic acid. Nearby was a slate on which the doctor had written a last note. It said that he had been in poor spirits for the past three weeks and added, 'I cannot bear the scandalous reports, goodbye to all. Distracted.'

The inquest was held at the *Halfway House* inn on Hessle Road and heard from Dr Muir who said that he was called to see Dr Stone at six-thirty in the morning. He was undressed, in bed and had been dead for some time as rigor mortis had set in. The doctor said that in the stomach he smelt some fluid which smelt of hydrocyanic acid, which had been the cause of death.

Mr Hart acted for the friends and family of the deceased man and said that looking back and knowing his keenness and sensitivity, and his impulsiveness, he could not say he was surprised that Dr Stone had taken his own life. It appeared to him as though he had come down to his surgery in the middle of the night after some sleepless hours in bed and took the acid on impulse, possibly distracted by a lack of sleep.

Mr Hart said that Dr Stone had ironically last been seen at an inquest the day before he was found and it was remarked by many there that he was looking pale and unwell.

The jury gave a verdict of suicide whilst of an unsound mind.

William Crapper

William Crapper, a watchmaker, aged forty-nine, had been in the asylum during the summer of 1900 due to melancholia and although he recovered sufficiently to live at home and continue with his trade, he had to be constantly monitored by family and friends to ensure his welfare.

On 20 March 1901, at about quarter to eight in the morning, Harriet Crapper, of West Parade in Hull, discovered William, lying on the floor of their bedroom with a silk handkerchief tied around his neck, suspended from the top rail of the bed. Her niece hurried to get a doctor and Dr Briggs soon arrived but there was nothing he could do for the man, who was already dead.

At the *Eagle Hotel*, Spring Bank, on Tuesday, 21 March, an inquiry was conducted into the circumstances surrounding his death and heard from Harriet, who confirmed that William had been an inmate at the Willerby Asylum and since that time he had been attended by Dr Gautby for mental derangement. For a month he had been confined to bed, though he had been watched closely.

The jury returned a verdict of suicide whilst of unsound mind.

Annie Foster

Annie Elizabeth Foster was a widow aged forty-nine who had been living with her stepbrother Edward Sayers at 24 Strickland Street since her husband died. She had been severely depressed since his death and Sayers, a labourer, was becoming increasingly worried about her. She was almost always in low spirits and had attempted to commit suicide on several other occasions.

He went to bed at ten o'clock on 27 November 1902 leaving her sitting by the fireside. He asked her to call him at six-thirty in the morning and she replied that she would if she was awake.

On 28 November he woke up and went to Annie's room to try and wake her. There was no response when he shouted for her so he went into the room where he was confronted with the sight of his step-sister hanging by a rope around her neck, suspended from a nail in the wall. Sayers rushed to the nearest police station for assistance and returned with a constable who cut the rope down and called Dr Fairbank, but he was only able to confirm that she was already dead.

An inquest was held into her death and the coroner asked Sayers if he had cut her down, Sayers replied no and the coroner asked why not. Sayers said, 'I dare not sir', to which the coroner said, 'But if you saw your sister drowning in the dock this morning wouldn't you have thrown her a rope?' Sayers replied, 'Oh, yes sir but I could not have cut her down this morning, she was quite cold.'

The coroner said that people who were not in the position that Sayers found himself that morning, could not reprimand him, but it was nevertheless a grave error that he did not cut her down as it could have saved her life. A verdict of suicide whilst temporarily insane was recorded.

Chapter 15

He Killed His Wife with a Razor 1908

Neighbours saw her stumble over the doorstep and into the street.

The marriage of Thomas and Gertrude Siddle was not a happy one. Thomas, a bricklayer, was twenty-nine years of age and had been married once before. Gertrude, seven years his junior, came from a respectable family and, though her family had doubts, decided to marry Thomas. The marriage produced two children, Harry aged fourteen months and Ethel, who was aged three.

Thomas had a long-standing drink problem though when clear of alcohol he appeared to have great affection for Gertrude and the children. The situation between the two of them deteriorated and grew to the point where it was beyond repair, leading to Gertrude and the two children moving out of the family home.

Due in large part to his drinking, Thomas came to be in debt and was arrested in May 1908, with Gertrude having applied for a warrant to force him into providing for her and the children. The magistrates gave him twenty-eight days in which to make good the account of £2 owing to his wife, otherwise he would go to prison for thirty days.

The 9 June 1908 was the 27th day of the order and towards dusk on that day, Siddle went to Strathfield House, Tyne Street, Hessle Road, which was where his wife and children had been living. The house was owned by Mabel Felcey who had befriended Gertrude and invited her to share her home. Gertrude and the children had been staying here for about five weeks.

Felcey opened the door when Siddle knocked. He asked for Gertie who was upstairs at the time. Mrs Felcey called her down saying, 'Gertie, here's your Tom.' She came downstairs and her husband entered the passage with Mrs Felcey a few

Many Edwardian working class families lived in crowded rooms.
Brian Elliott Collection

feet away. Gertrude was wearing a wedding ring and Thomas wanted to know where it had come from as it was not given to her by him. Mrs Felcey said that she had brought the ring for Gertrude who reassured her estranged husband that no man had bought it for her. She said that she had given Mrs Felcey a shilling for it.

Thomas said to Gertrude, 'I've come to say goodbye, I'm going up the road for thirty days for not paying the money I should have done.' By this he meant that he would be going to prison. Gertie said that she was sorry and told him to make a man of himself. He added, 'Well Gerty, I will get a regular job when I get out and get a good home and live happier. This game cannot last forever. The children are getting older.' The couple talked for a little while longer and Siddle concluded by saying, 'Ta ta Gert, I'm going to shake hands.'

However, as she went to shake hands he made a grab for her wrists and chased her into the passage before whipping a razor from his pocket and cutting her throat twice, inflicting massive wounds. Gertie shouted 'Oh Mabel!' and fell in a heap on the floor, blood flowing from the wounds. Felcey rushed from the house shouting 'Murder!' Neighbours saw her stumble over the doorstep and into the street. Siddle was also seen, blood on his hands and the razor visible in his right hand. He muttered 'God forgive me,' but stayed in the area of the house and did not attempt to run away.

A crowd soon gathered and whilst some went to fetch a policeman, others escorted the dying woman to the chemist's shop on the corner of Dee Street on Hessle Road. John Suddaby, the chemist, dressed Gertrude's wounds but, seeing that the injuries she had sustained were so serious, told those with her that she must get hospital treatment immediately. By this time PC Taylor arrived, leaving Gertrude with PC Field who flagged down a parcels delivery van which took her to the Royal Infirmary. However, it was to be in vain as Gertie died fifteen minutes after admission to the hospital.

Taylor meanwhile went in search of Siddle, soon catching up with him near the scene of the murder. Thomas Siddle was removed to the central police station in Parliament Street before being remanded in Hedon Road prison.

Gertie's funeral was held on 13 June at the Western Cemetery and a large crowd gathered around the house in Tyne Street, on Hessle Road, along the Boulevard and Walton Street, comprising mostly of women and children. It was said that no such crowd had been seen at the cemetery since the burials of the victims of the North Sea tragedy. The coffin could be seen through the glass of the hearse, covered with violet velvet and with silver fittings. It bore an inscription on the breastplate, 'Gertrude Siddle, died June 9 1908 aged 22.'

The *Hull Times* reported that the tragedy had touched even children, quoting one little girl as saying, to another on St George's Road, 'I'm going to see the poor lady buried,' with her friend responding, 'Hey let's go early.'

People started arriving at the cemetery shortly after noon although the fact that it was dinner time delayed many until almost one-thirty. The *Hull Times* added:

> *Husband's dinners must be cooked and the diligent wives hurried away when their duties were done. Mrs Hessle Road was well represented. She always hastens to show her sympathy when it is deserved and such was certainly the case in the present instance. Police were also evident in the funeral procession.*

Tragically, there were two young children who had been left without a mother as a result of the murder. They had been cared for in the Beverley Road workhouse, but their long-term future was very uncertain with their mother dead and their father due to stand trial and facing a possible death sentence.

Siddle was due to stand trial for murder at the York Assizes in July 1908 although observers of his behaviour in prison said that he hardly seemed to realise the position in which he was placed.

His parents lived in abject poverty in a terrace in Gibson Street and Siddle remained close to them up until the end. During his incarceration awaiting trial Siddle had written letters to his parents, one of them saying he could not tell what had come over him on the fateful night and he hoped that God might forgive him. A few days before being taken to York for the

Getting clean in the workhouse. Brian Elliott Collection

trial, he wrote further, enquiring as to the future of his children and his father who had visited him in Hedon Road Gaol.

At York Assizes, counsel for the prosecution told how Siddle had failed to provide for his wife and children during their life together and how an order was taken out against him to force him into paying maintenance allowance to his wife. No money was paid and on the day of the crime, Siddle arrived at the house in Tyne Street. He told his estranged wife that he was going down the road for the non-payment of the order, meaning that he would be taken into custody and that it would make a man of him.

Counsel said that the attack happened when Gertrude was off her guard and pointed out that the jury would have no difficulty coming to the conclusion that Siddle knew what he was doing at the time the crime took place. He was not drunk and there was no apparent motive. He came to the house with a razor, the inference being that he came with a pre-meditated intention to kill her.

Mabel Felcey, giving evidence for the prosecution, described the tragedy and said that Thomas Siddle had pawned his wife's original wedding ring for 1s 6d which was why she had given her a replacement. On the attack itself, she said that the incident had happened so quickly that she had not seen it take

York Minster and the city walls in the early 1900s. Brian Elliott Collection

place but she did see Gertrude on the floor, with Thomas holding her by the wrist. He added that Gertrude's throat had been cut right across and she then ran into the street shrieking and pleading for assistance to try and help her friend.

PC Taylor said Siddle had gone up to him and said, 'I give myself up for the murder of my wife.' Another witness, Carl Michael, handed the police officer the razor, which had been found on the floor. Seeing this, Siddle said, 'Take care of it, that is what I did it with.'

Siddle went into the witness box on his own behalf and said that on the date of the murder he had had nothing to eat and had been drinking for nine weeks without eating anything.

On the murder he told the court that, 'Something came over me. I do not know what it was I only realised what I had done when the blood was on my hand. I had no intention of killing my wife. I liked my wife and the children too well.' He explained that he had borrowed the razor from his father in order that a friend might shave him.

Mr Hamilton, on Siddle's behalf, read a letter from Dr Horton of Hull Gaol which stated that Siddle, during his time in the prison, had shown signs of chronic alcoholism but that his condition had improved and he was now of a sound mind. Mr Hamilton asked for a recommendation for mercy on account of Siddle's youth and appealed to the jury that they may find him not guilty of murder but guilty of manslaughter. However, the jury ignored this advice and, after a short deliberation, returned to court to find him guilty of murder, with the judge passing the death sentence.

The *Hull Times* reported the trial and the effect it was having on the people of Hessle Road. The newspaper said:

> *All Hessle Road cried out with horror and indignation when they learnt how Thomas Siddle, after asking to shake hands with his wife in a passage at Strathfield House, Tyne Street, Hull turned upon her with an open razor and cut her throat with such force and ferocity that her life sped in a brief while.*

When the train carrying Siddle arrived back at Paragon Station a large number of people gathered around the platform. He rushed through them and heard good luck messages as well as some wanting to 'Hang the murderer.'

Siddle's father sprung into action to try and earn his son a reprieve and, in the days immediately after the trial, he spent most of his time writing to MPs and the Home Secretary. He soon received a reply from the Home Office to say that the Home Secretary was currently considering the matter. His father also managed to secure 3,500 signatures for a petition which was also sent to the Home Secretary.

However, a few days later all hope vanished when a letter came back from the Home Secretary saying that after considering the matter, there were no grounds on which he was able to interfere and the law would have to take its course. It was a bitter blow to Siddle and his father who both hoped and believed that his youth may have led to a different outcome.

Siddle was reportedly in a state verging on collapse during the latter stages of his incarceration before going to the gallows. He was said to be bearing up badly and had to be force fed. All hope left him as he realised that there was no hope of the reprieve efforts succeeding. The night before his execution he expressed penitence for his deed as his fate lay heavily upon him. Siddle was duly executed in accordance with the death sentence.

Paragon Square and the Cenotaph, Hull (from an old picture postcard).
David Goodman Collection

On the eve of his execution Siddle wrote to his parents:

This is the last letter that you will ever get from me, cheer up and don't trouble about me as it is not troubling me as I am hoping to go to a better place where I hope to see my two wives in heaven and where I hope to meet you all. I'm only sorry to think what trouble I have brought upon you all and upon my poor little children. Look what a disgrace it will be to them when they grow up to have on their minds that their mother was murdered by their father (which I have admitted to) and that I was hanged, executed by the law, but I hope and trust to the Lord I am the last one of our family to have to meet such an awful death as that I have to suffer for it would never have happened at all. It was all through that cursed drink that I have given up all worldly matters and I'm now ready to meet my maker. When you come for my bit of property there is a little testament which you want to give to my little daughter Jeanie. It was a present to me by a gentleman which I read and I hope she will do the same and I know she will keep Sarah's photo. As for little Ethel I want her to go to my cousin Susanna at Grimsby as she will be better off in that town than in Hull as she will know nothing about her parents.

Hull's Market Place looks busy in this Edwardian postcard, posted in 1906.
David Goodman Collection

Bibliography

Young, Angus, *Murders of Hull*, 1996

Young, Angus, *More Murders of Hull, Capital Crimes*, 1997

Goodman, David, *Aspects of Hull*, 1999

Wrigglesworth, Edmund, *Brown's Illustrated Guide to Hull*, 1992

Markham, John, *Centenary Book of Hull*, 1997

Hull Daily Mail, *Hull - The Fishing Years*, 1999

Clarke AA, *Policemen of Hull*, 1992

Hull Daily Mail

Hull News

Hull Times

Hull Packet

Yorkshire Post

Index